Irish Indoor Insects

A Guide to Irish Indoor Insect Pests

Irish Indoor Insects

A Guide to Irish Indoor Insect Pests

James P O'Connor

&

Patrick Ashe

Illustrations by Sean Milne

TOWN
HOUSE
DUBLIN

First published in 2000 by

Town House & Country House Ltd.
Trinity House, Charleston Rd
Ranelagh, Dublin 6

ISBN: 1–86059–095–0

A CIP catalogue record for this book is available from the British Library.

Cover illustrations by Sean Milne
Cover design by Jason Ellams

Typeset by Typeform Repro, Dublin

Printed in Spain by Estudios Gráficos ZURE S.A.

Dedication

This book is dedicated to the memory of our late friend Dr Norman Hickin (1910–90). He was one of those rare geniuses in life who combined talent with enthusiasm and good humour. It was always a great pleasure to meet him.

Born in Aston, Birmingham, he reared out his first wood-boring insect when he was only sixteen years of age and subsequently became a world authority on pest insects, particularly woodworm. He worked for Rentokil for nearly thirty years and became their scientific director.

A prolific researcher and author, he wrote numerous books and scientific papers. These deal with an impressive range of subjects, including household pests, the natural history of an English forest, caddis larvae, the insect factor in wood decay, an African notebook, beachcombing for beginners and the animal life of the Galapagos Islands. Many were illustrated with his magnificent scraper-board drawings.

In later life, Norman became very fond of Ireland. He was a frequent visitor and spent much of his time here. Indeed, his last book was a comprehensive field guide to Irish butterflies which was published after his death.

Contents

Acknowledgements

This book is a compilation based on the authors' experience and on data contained in the books and scientific papers listed in the references. During the ten years we spent in writing it, numerous people provided encouragement. Many entomological, zoological and other friends read drafts or gave freely of their knowledge and expertise. In particular, we would like to thank Ken and Vera Smith, who painstakingly corrected our English and made many valuable improvements in the text. We would also wish to thank Tom Bolger, Ken Bond, Fidelma Butler, Jervis Good, Mark Holmes, Mike Morris, Declan Murray, Robert Nash, Brian Nelson, Robert Nelson, Mary O'Connor, David Pinniger, Jim Ryan, Paddy Sleeman and Stuart Wistow. We are indebted to Dr P.F. Wallace, Director of the National Museum of Ireland, for providing a preface.

The book was undertaken as a hobby during our spare time and the staff of two marvellous Dublin public houses helped us by providing congenial surroundings, excellent Guinness and often even a 'snug' all to ourselves. We are very grateful to the following for all their kindness: Kevin Fitzimons, owner of Fitzsimons' (formerly Kennedy's) of Westland Row, and the former Kennedy's staff members Pat Brogan (manager), Gabriel Corless (assistant manager), Paul Andrews, Martin Darcy, Joe Dillon, Colin Durkan, Paddy Durkan, Des Hayes, Ann Hetherton, Dermot Kilbride, Ken Knowles and John Paul O'Brien; Frank Quinn, owner of Toner's of Baggot Street, and his staff Paul Corcoran (manager), Jim Costello, Martin Flatley, Pat Hopkins, Tom Kerrigan and Billy Ryan.

Special thanks to our publisher Treasa Coady for her interest in and support of this project, to Dr Siobhán Parkinson who did a marvellous job of editing the text; to the artist Sean Milne for his superb illustrations; to the National Museum of Ireland for a contribution towards the cost of publication; to the Heritage Council for helpful advice; and André Deutsch Ltd. for permission to use the Ogden Nash poems.

National Museum of Ireland
Ard-Mhúsaem na hÉireann

Foreword

Although quite genuinely fascinated by and mostly sympathetic to insects and their study—particularly by an enthusiast (most avowedly not an apologist) like my colleague Dr Jim O'Connor—I can hardly be described as an entomologist, even by the most generously amateur definition. Nevertheless, I feel Dr O'Connor has accorded me a great honour in asking me to introduce this work. As head of the National Museum, I have ultimate responsibility for the insect collection which Jim O'Connor has single-handedly done so much to expand, and this is one reason I have been asked to write these few paragraphs. I suspect another reason is that he has so often had to listen to my pleas that he write something general for the widest audience about his beloved subject—which he most assuredly does here—that he senses that I too am, at heart, fascinated by insects and their behaviour. And he is right.

My first realisation of the scientific value of insect study to my own principal passion—early medieval urbanism—was G. C. Coope's brilliant essay in the *Proceedings of the Eighth Viking Congress*. In this discussion of insect remains from Dublin's Viking houses, Coope showed that not only could insects give us a good idea of the food detritus which lay around the floors of such buildings, but their sensitivity to temperature could actually allow us to reconstruct the atmosphere of thousand-year-old houses.

And there was more. Here were discoveries that history itself would never even mention. This essay was followed by Dr O'Connor's own discussion of the implications of the finding of a couple of *Blaps* on the Fishamble Street excavations (see page 67)—implications about commerce and external contact and about environmental conditions. As with my interest in animal bones, I was immediately smitten by insect students, particularly Jim O'Connor and Paddy Ashe, whose company I have all too rarely relished.

Over the years, I have, in the parlance of zoologists, 'captured' several insects. (Actually I have usually confined them to a matchbox where they were suffocated and starved into specimen-elect condition, but zoologists describe scraping an unfortunate insect into a biro case or matchbox as a 'capture' as if they were talking about the set of *The African Queen* rather than a living room or, in a legendary O'Connor and Ashe instance, the men's room of a Dublin public house.) These specimens I have passed on to Jim for identification, in the hope that not only might I add to the collections and the stock of information by finding a new species, but also in the hope that he might accept my *bona fides* as a proto-amateur entomologist, more a poacher or big game hunter (the zoologist's equivalent of the archaeologist's nemesis—the treasure hunter!) than a zoologist.

Having failed with silverfish and different types of ants (always getting wonderful replies telling me about the characteristics of my 'capture'), I finally struck it rich in the summer of 1996, when I was taken by a strange-looking 'bug', which Jim O'Connor told me had never before been noted in Dublin city. In addition, all the existing museum specimens were over one hundred and fifty years old. Success at last and a shot in the arm to go on deluging my unfortunate colleague in natural history. Thanks to Dr O'Connor, a scientific paper on my discovery now has my name tagged on as a co-author, in an area of the National Museum where I never dreamed I would ever publish anything. Genuine ecstasy (of the old variety)!

My respect for insects has been fully restored from my earliest memory of them as flies, wasps, honey bees and dungbeetles. Flies I remember half stuck and struggling on fly papers in Mrs Foley's pub in Askeaton almost forty years ago. And my mother's failure to believe that a squirt of Cooper's fly-spray would have done the job as well as the car wash proportions she drowned her unfortunate victims in. One terrible wasp I recall as having been stuck on to a jam knife wielded by a farmer visiting our home, who immediately whipped it to the floor, where it survived, semi-paralysed but well enough to sting me badly as I played on the floor some time later. Honey bees for the seemingly ridiculous garb which my uncle used to don when dealing with swarming bees or retrieving honey from his hives. And this to be followed by the inevitable lecture on how good honey was for you and that he would never get arthritis, so many stings had he had. He didn't. Unfortunately he died of something else altogether! Dung beetles were part of life at the forge with their auburn colour lit by sunlight making them indistinguishable from their feast—or should that be their raison d'être? One recalls too the scourge of the warble and the consternation they caused farmers, the messing of schoolfriends with horseflies, the viciousness of midges and the uncanny knack ticks had of finding the softest part of your body as you sat in a meadow, on a bog or at the roadside.

Insects were certainly everywhere in our youth. They still are. Sometimes they are unfriendly and can even kill. Mostly, however, they are our friends and it is in that positive spirit that they have been studied by O'Connor and Ashe.

And let us just reflect lastly on how much a part of our lives and culture they have become. Italian scooters are called Vespas (or wasps) for the obvious reason, the Volkswagen was called a beetle and a bug, grasshoppers are names for aircraft, the Beatles and their inspirers the Crickets have had chart successes—and it is not that long since we used to try to dance the Fly. I cannot remember attempting the Jitterbug but I do know that James Dean was killed driving a Porsche 'Spyder'. And who has not wished to be a fly on the wall? And that beautiful Irish admonition—*Aithníonn ciaróg*

ciaróg eile (literally 'One beetle recognises another'), which means it takes one to know one! I can recognise and salute good work presented to a popular audience and I commend and thank Jim O'Connor and Paddy Ashe for so doing and for letting us all be flies on their walls.

Patrick F Wallace, Director, National Museum of Ireland
March 1997

Preface

We hope that this book will be unique both in helping people with their insect problems and in promoting a love of insects. It is based on our practical experiences as Irish entomologists who have by accident become involved with solving people's insect problems, because of a scarcity of entomologists in Ireland. We both very much enjoy working on the wild or non-pest insects but once people realised that we could also identify the pest species, we became inundated with requests for assistance, and it has been a very rewarding and worthwhile experience. As a result of the numerous enquiries we have received, we realised the need for a book on the indoor pest insects of Ireland and this volume was written to cater for this need.

For the last twenty years, we have been interested in pest species and this book is based on our experiences. It is intended to help members of the public, health and agricultural inspectors and other non-entomologists to identify and eradicate most pest insects found indoors. It will be of particular interest to those employed in the food industry. Information is given on previous Irish records and life-histories. We have also included some harmless insects which are frequently found in houses. The illustrations of the various species are based on a combination of the skill and interpretation of the artist Sean Milne, and an examination of numerous existing drawings, sketches and preserved museum specimens by the authors, with corrections where necessary, to ensure accuracy.

When rural science was abolished in Irish schools in the 1930s to make more time for studying the Irish language, generations of Irish people missed out on learning about insects. Nature study has, fortunately, since been reintroduced, but the syllabus does not include much about insects, and the result is that most people in this country know very little about insects and many are afraid of them. We wish to allay people's fears about insects with this book, by indicating which ones are harmful and which not.

The majority of pests included in this book are those which are most likely to be encountered indoors or which cause problems for individuals. Only a few are medically harmful.

James P O'Connor
Patrick Ashe
October 1998

Chapter 1: Identifying Insects

On the Beauty of Insects

Observe the insect race, ordain'd to keep
The lazy sabbath of a half year's sleep.
Entomb'd beneath the filmy web they lie,
And wait the influence of a kinder sky.

Anon.[1]

As an island isolated from the European mainland, Ireland has only a limited vertebrate fauna (mammals, birds, fish, amphibians and reptiles). By contrast, however, there is an amazing variety of insects here and already some 16,000 species are known. Happily, most are harmless and live their lives without adversely affecting Irish people, their animals or their crops. Indeed, some predators and scavengers are highly beneficial, while the pollinators are vital to human survival. However, a small percentage (2%) are pests and do cause problems. Some are mere nuisances, but others are responsible for serious economic damage or are health hazards.

What is an Insect?

Many people confuse insects with other small creatures such as spiders, mites, ticks, millipedes, woodlice and so on. To clarify the situation, the key characters for recognising an insect are given here.

The adult insect

1. It has six legs.
2. The body is divided into three distinct parts:
   - a head at the front with eyes, feelers (antennae) and mouthparts
   - a thorax in the middle with the six legs and usually one or two pairs of wings (though some species are wingless)
   - an abdomen at the back, which may be soft or hard, and carries the sex organs

1 *Quoted from* The Natural History of Remarkable Insects with their habits and instincts, *William de Veaux,* Dublin, 1819 *(probably edited by Rev Charles Bardin)*

1

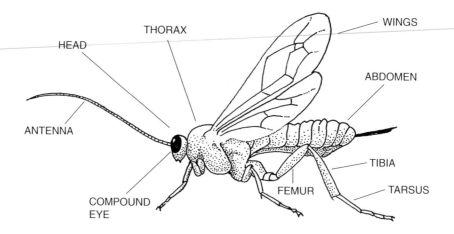

There may be other structures that are part of the abdomen, such as 'tails' or a sting. Many beetles have hardened front wings, which may cover most of the abdomen from above.

The immature insect

Most female insects lay eggs, but some can produce live young. As might be expected, the eggs are normally very small and difficult to find or identify (with a few exceptions, we have not included them in this book).

After the egg stage, insects may have one of two different types of development, namely *incomplete* and *complete metamorphosis.*

Complete metamorphosis occurs with the more advanced groups of insects such as fleas, lacewings, beetles, flies, butterflies, moths, bees and wasps. The insect goes through a series of stages from egg to adult insect, and at each stage the creature looks completely different. The hatching insect (*larva*) looks nothing like the adult. It feeds and moults, growing each time. When fully mature, it changes into a *pupa* or *chrysalis,*[2] where its tissues are reorganised and the adult structures develop. When this process is completed, the adult insect breaks out of the pupal skin and completes the life-cycle – in other words, it is now ready to mate and produce offspring of its own. Once the adult emerges from the pupa it is fully grown: it does not moult and a small butterfly cannot grow into a bigger butterfly.

Generally more primitive insects, such as grasshoppers, crickets, cockroaches, earwigs, booklice and lice, have *incomplete metamorphosis,* in other words, they grow from an egg into an adult

2 Pupae are not described in this book, only adult insects and larvae, as the pupal stage may last only a short time, is rarely seen and is difficult to identify

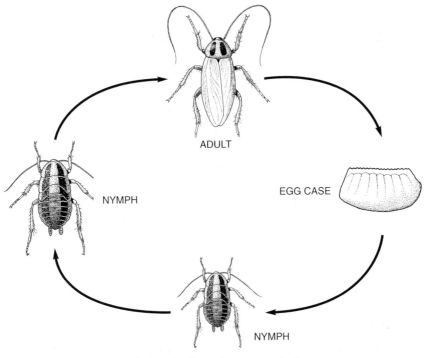

ADULT

NYMPH

EGG CASE

NYMPH

Cockroach – Incomplete metamorphosis

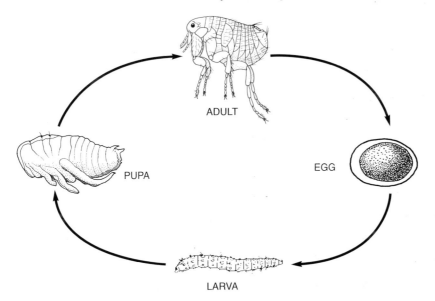

ADULT

PUPA

EGG

LARVA

Flea – Complete metamorphosis

without going through the larval and pupal stages. The hatching insect or *nymph* is a miniature version of the adult. Depending on the species, the young insect moults or casts its skin a number of times, increasing in size until it reaches that of the adult. It then becomes sexually mature and can complete the life-cycle.

Pest Larvae

Larvae of some insects, such as bluebottles and houseflies, do not have an obvious head and these larvae are often called *maggots*. Beetle larvae are frequently known as *grubs*, and those of moths and butterflies as *caterpillars*. Apart from maggots, larvae usually have a distinct head, which is darker in colour than the body.

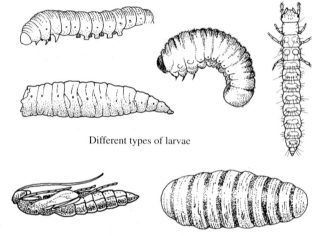

Different types of larvae

Different types of pupae

Most larvae tend to be elongated and worm-like in shape but other forms do occur, including some bizarre ones. Like the adult, the body of a larva is divided into a head, thorax and abdomen, but these divisions may not be obvious, and wings are completely absent.

Three pairs of jointed legs may be present on the thorax but they are much smaller and less well developed than in the adult. Some may have additional unjointed tube-like legs on the abdomen, as in the caterpillars of moths and butterflies. However, in many fly larvae and some beetle grubs, legs may be completely absent.

Larvae that hide from the light in food or other materials are normally white or pale-coloured. Ones that do not avoid light are often camouflaged or darker in colour. There may be warning colours or some form of defence.

Classifying and Naming Insects

All insects are placed together in a group known as the Class Insecta. This is divided into a number of distinct sections called 'orders' which include many of the familiar natural groupings: beetles (Order Coleoptera), flies (Order Diptera) and moths and butterflies (Order Lepidoptera). There are about thirty different orders but only some members of them cause problems indoors in Ireland.

Orders are further subdivided, but in general the only other classifications used in this book are family, genus and species. As the name implies, all the species in a particular family are closely related to one another. Zoologists, whether studying insects or any other group, have come to use a simple, standardised method of naming species, which has the advantage of being completely international and understandable by all.

Example: *Stegobium paniceum* (Linnaeus)

This scientific name consists of two Latin or latinised words printed in italics, the first word beginning with a capital letter, the second not. The first part of the name (*Stegobium* in the example) shows the genus (which is a subdivision of a family) to which the insect belongs, and the second part (*paniceum* in the example) identifies the particular species. The name of the person who first described the species (known as the authority) is given after the species name, in ordinary roman type and sometimes enclosed in brackets,[3] and again this name begins with a capital letter.

Scientific names are used throughout the book as they will enable interested readers to discover more about any particular species in the list of references. However, where possible, common English names are also given. These are not universal, however, even in English-speaking areas, and other 'common names' may exist elsewhere in the world or indeed in different parts of Ireland and Britain. Different names may also be used in other languages. For example, *Stegobium paniceum* (Linnaeus) is called the biscuit beetle (in Britain and Ireland), the drug store beetle (in the USA), *vrillette du pain* (in France), *Brotkäfer* (in Germany) and *carcoma del pan* (in Spain). (Irish names are provided in Appendix 4.)

Guide to Identifying Insect Orders

The identification guide provided here is designed to help you to identify your specimen as easily as possible. Simply match the insect to the illustration which most closely resembles it, taking into account the size range and the diagnostic features. When you have found the appropriate order,

3 If there are brackets, this means that the person who first identified and described the insect originally put it in a different genus from the one it is now assigned to

then consult the relevant chapter. If you cannot decide, it may help to flick through the illustrations in the various chapters.

Order	Size range (excludes length of antennae or 'tails')	Diagnostic features
COLLEMBOLA (Springtails: Ch 2)	5mm or less	Wingless; cylindrical or round body; white, bluish or blackish; forked spring-like 'tail' enables it to hop; small insects, often found in damp places (e.g. around sinks) Immature stages: resemble adults, except smaller

Springtail – Collembola

| **THYSANURA** (Silverfish and firebrat: Ch 2) | 11–12mm | Wingless; carrot-shaped body; silvery; three long 'tails'; medium-sized insects, often seen when light is switched on at night Immature stages: resemble adults, except smaller |

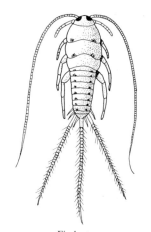

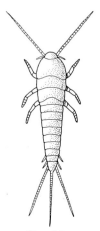

Firebrat –
Thermobia domestica
(Packard)

Silverfish –
Lepisma saccharina
(Linnaeus)

Order	Size range (excludes length of antennae or 'tails')	Diagnostic features

BLATTODEA
(Cockroaches: Ch 2)

10–43mm

Winged (usually two pairs, first leathery, covering second, membranous pair; wings occasionally reduced); flattened, oval body; six well-developed, similarly sized, spiky legs; antennae long and whip-like; two short cerci or 'tails'; medium to large insects, sometimes mistaken for beetles; usually active at night and run quickly across floors or walls when disturbed; rarely fly

Immature stages: resemble adults, except smaller

Common Cockroach –
Blatta orientalis
Linnaeus

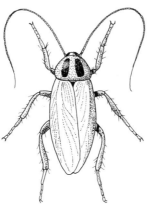

German Cockroach –
Blattella germanica
(Linnaeus)

ORTHOPTERA
(Crickets and grasshoppers: Ch 2)

11–80mm

Usually winged (two pairs, first leathery, covering second, membranous pair); occasionally wingless; cylindrical, narrow body; hind legs enlarged for jumping; antennae usually long and whip-like; 'tails' present or absent; medium to large insects

Immature stages: resemble adults, except smaller

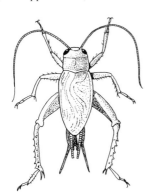

House Cricket –
Acheta domestica
(Linnaeus)

Egyptian Grasshopper –
Anacridium aegyptium
(Linnaeus)

Order	Size range (excludes length of antennae or 'tails')	Diagnostic features
DERMAPTERA (Earwigs: Ch 2)	12–20mm	Winged (two pairs, first, small and scale-like, protect the large, membranous second pair) but seldom flies; flattened, elongated body; dark brown; legs short; tip of abdomen has unmistakable pincers or forceps; medium to large insects

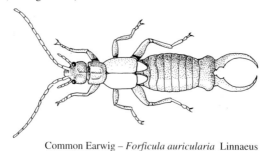

Common Earwig – *Forficula auricularia* Linnaeus

Immature stages: resemble adults, except smaller

| **PSOCOPTERA** (Booklice: Ch 2) | 1–3mm | Winged (two pairs, both membranous, held tent-like over body when at rest; wings often reduced) or wingless; flattened, egg-shaped body; whitish to dark brown; very small insects, often mistaken for mites; frequently found amongst books or papers, as small moving dots. |

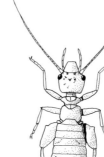

Bark Louse – Psocoptera

Immature stages: resemble adults, except smaller

Book Louse – Psocoptera

Order	Size range (excludes length of antennae or 'tails')	Diagnostic features

PHTHIRAPTERA

(Lice: Ch 2)

1–4mm

Wingless; external parasites of mammals and birds; flattened body; whitish to brown (reddish after blood meal); legs stout, with strong claws for gripping hair or feathers of host; very small insects

Immature stages: resemble adults, except smaller

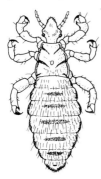

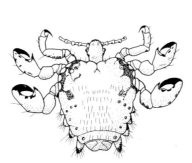

Head Louse –
Pediculus humanus
var *capitis*
De Geer

Crab Louse –
Pthirus pubis
(Linnaeus)

THYSANOPTERA

(Thrips: Ch 2)

1–7mm

Winged (two pairs, both narrow, fringed with long hairs) or wingless; body slender and elongated; reddish or black; legs short; very small or small insects, most frequently found on fresh vegetables (e.g. lettuce)

Immature stages: resemble adults, except smaller

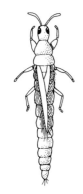

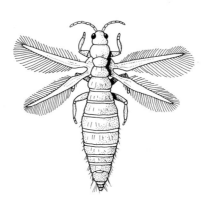

Thrips – Thysanoptera

9

Order	Size range (excludes length of antennae or 'tails')	Diagnostic features

SIPHONAPTERA
(Fleas: Ch 2)

1–8mm

Wingless; external parasites of mammals and birds; body round or oval, flattened sideways; reddish to black (due to blood feeding); legs strongly developed for jumping, with long claws for gripping hair or feathers of host; very small to small insects, mostly found on host, in clothing, bedding or nests

Immature stages: larva and pupa completely unlike adults

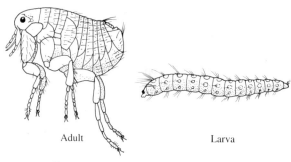

Adult   Larva

Plague Flea – *Xenopsylla cheopis* (Rothschild)

NEUROPTERA
(Lacewings: Ch 2)

10–13mm

Winged (two pairs, both large, transparent, with numerous veins and cells, held tent-like over body when at rest); body smaller than a single wing, long and slender, tapering up towards tip of abdomen; pale green to brown; legs weakly developed, slender, medium-sized insects, often found indoors, hibernating for winter

Immature stages: larva and pupa completely unlike adults, larva with well-developed mouthparts—predators

Green Lacewing – *Chrysopa (Chrysoperla) carnea* Stephens

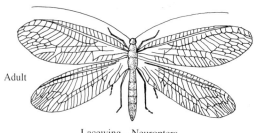

Adult

Lacewing – Neuroptera

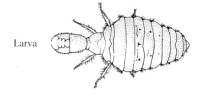

Larva

Order	Size range (excludes length of antennae or 'tails')	Diagnostic features
HEMIPTERA (Bugs, aphids, whiteflies, scale insects: Ch 3)	1–16mm	Winged (two pairs, either both pairs membranous (as in aphids) or first pair opaque at base and membranous at tip and second pair completely membranous, or rarely only one pair (e.g. male scale insects) or wingless (including some aphids)); needle- like piercing mouthparts, located on the underside of the head (can easily be pulled down with a pin); mostly feed on plant juices with a few blood-feeding species; very small to large insects

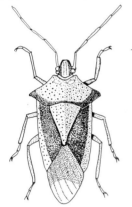

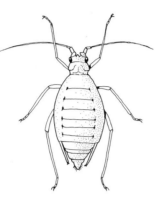

Hawthorn Shield Bug –
Acanthosoma haemorrhoidale
(Linnaeus)

Wingless Greenfly –
Aphididae

Immature stages: mostly resemble
small adults though some (e.g.
whiteflies) have a nymph and
pupal stage which are completely
unlike adults

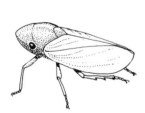

Froghopper –
Hemiptera

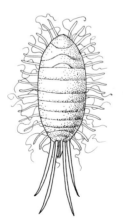

Mealy Bug –
Pseudococcus sp

Order	**Size range** (excludes length of antennae or 'tails')	**Diagnostic features**

COLEOPTERA
(Beetles: Ch 4)

1–35mm

Winged (two pairs, first hard, opaque and shell-like, which cover and hide the second membranous pair used for flying; first pair may be greatly reduced; second pair sometimes reduced or lost); body usually sturdy and compact, with a hard 'skin'; legs usually well developed, often with strong claws, spines or enlarged joints; very small to very large insects

Varied Carpet Beetle –
Anthrenus verbasci
(Linnaeus)
Adult

Cockchafer –
Melolontha melolontha
(Linnaeus)
Adult

Fly-in-the-Eye Beetle –
Anotylus tetracarinatus
(Block)

Immature stages: larva and pupa completely unlike adults

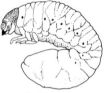

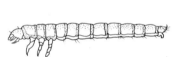

Yellow Mealworm Beetle –
Tenebrio molitor (Linnaeus)
Larva

Cockchafer –
Melolontha melolontha
(Linnaeus)
Larva

DIPTERA
(Flies: Ch 5)

1–65mm

Winged (one pair of membranous, transparent wings, sometimes with spots or pattern, rarely very hairy (e.g. moth flies), wings sometimes reduced or lost); pair of knobbed rod-like balancing organs (very reduced wings) located near base of wings; antennae usually short and indistinct, sometimes long and thread-like or bushy; legs usually long and slender; very small to very large insects.

Stable Fly –
Stomoxys calcitrans
(Linnaeus)

Order	Size range (excludes length of antennae or 'tails')	Diagnostic features	

DIPTERA – *continued*

Immature stages: larva and pupa completely unlike adults

House Fly Maggot – *Musca domestica* Linnaeus
Larva

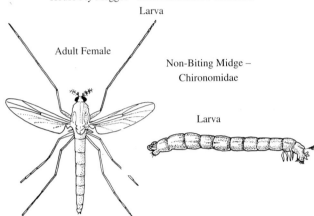

Adult Female

Non-Biting Midge –
Chironomidae

Larva

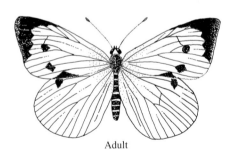

LEPIDOPTERA   7–130mm

(Butterflies and moths: Ch 6)

Winged (two pairs, both usually of similar size, opaque and covered in scales (easily rubbed off and like a fine dust when touched) which can vary greatly in colour often creating a distinct pattern); body long and slender, also covered in scales; antennae with many segments, often comb-like (clubbed in butterflies); small to very large insects

Immature stages: larva (caterpillar) and pupa (chrysalis) completely unlike adults

Adult

Large White Butterfly – *Pieris brassicae* (Linnaeus)

Caterpillar

Order	Size range (excludes length of antennae or 'tails')	Diagnostic features
HYMENOPTERA (Ants, bees and wasps: Ch 7)	1–51mm	Winged (two pairs, membranous, sometimes with distinct spot, second pair usually much smaller than first, both pairs linked together with small hooks) or wingless (e.g. many ants); body often has a distinct narrow waist between thorax and abdomen; antennae often long with many segments or elbowed (e.g. ants); some species create nests of many individuals and different castes (e.g. queen, drone, worker) and many are internal parasites of other insects; females often have long sting-like egg-laying ovipositor which is modified into a sting in some species; very small to very large insects

Immature stages: larva and pupa rarely seen and completely unlike adults |

Honey Bee – *Apis mellifera* Linnaeus
Adult

Ant – Formicidae

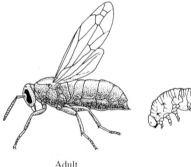

Adult

Larva

Sawfly – Symphyta

Chapter 2: The Smaller Insect Orders

Their song in the great heat here has the same charm for
me as the cricket on the hearth of the peasants at home.

Vincent van Gogh writing about cicadas to his brother Theo
(letter of 2 July 1889)

Springtails   Order: Collembola

Springtails are cylindrical or round wingless insects, usually less than 5mm long. Although mostly grey or brown, white, black, mottled and other colours do exist. A distinctive feature is the presence of a forked spring-like tail which is normally folded under the body. When released, it allows the insect to jump into the air. The young stages resemble the adults.

Springtail – Collembola

Outdoors, they live in soil, leaf litter and decaying vegetable matter where they are important in converting such material into substances for use by other life forms. They prefer moist, humid conditions and low temperatures (3°C to 15°C). Indoors, their presence is usually symptomatic of dampness. They can occur around sinks and drains (especially in kitchens and bathrooms), in side passages, damp cellars, in pot plants or other situations with moist conditions and decomposing or rotting plant material. Indeed, since they feed on fungi, they will occur where moulds are found. Large numbers of a white species can occur with potted plants.

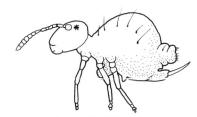

Springtail – Collembola

They are not considered a health hazard and do not bite. However if touched or disturbed, they will hop short distances while searching for a new hiding place. Such behaviour can alarm people who may mistake the springtails for fleas. In addition, they can contaminate foodstuffs.

Thysanurans (Silverfish and Firebrat)   Order: Thysanura

With their silvery appearance, wingless carrot-shaped body, long antennae and three tails, these primitive insects are easily recognised. Shy creatures, they are normally only noticed by people when using bathrooms or kitchens at night.

Silverfish   *Lepisma saccharina* (Linnaeus)

The mature insect is about 11–12mm long (excluding antennae and tails). The popular name derives from the tiny silvery scales which cover the body. Unknown in any habitat in the open, it is purely a domestic creature and has probably lived in human dwellings for several thousand years. Indeed, it was mentioned in a Chinese dictionary over two thousand years ago.

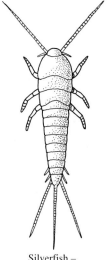

Only a small number of eggs (average about fifty) are laid and the mother carefully looks after them. The newly hatched nymphs (c. 2mm) resemble their parents. Silverfish moult throughout their life and a lost leg can be regrown. Individuals may live for seven years, a considerable length of time for an insect.

Mainly feeding on protein or carbohydrate-rich foods (such as bread, cereals, flour, starch, sugar, glues and pastes on wallpaper and books), they like warm (22°–32°C) humid conditions. They are active at night and are often noticed in a kitchen or bathroom when the light is switched

Silverfish –
Lepisma saccharina
(Linnaeus)

on, causing them to run for cover. They are clean and odourless animals and, since they normally cause little damage in houses, many naturalists consider them welcome guests in their homes, even rescuing them from their commonest trap—the bath. They can be a pest, though, in large numbers in bakeries, libraries and food factories, where they can contaminate goods.

Occasionally, individuals enter open packets of food in cupboards and are trapped. When a silverfish is discovered by a householder while, for example, pouring cornflakes, the manufacturer may be erroneously blamed. One of us was called in on one occasion to give an opinion where a specimen appeared in a bottle of tonic in Dublin – clearly an incident of this type.

Firebrat   *Thermobia domestica* (Packard)

Resembling the silverfish, the firebrat is greyish and about 11mm in length (not including antennae and tails) when mature. There are very few Irish records and it was first reported as recently as 1932. As the name implies, this species likes heat, ideally 32°–41°C—a temperature range much warmer than the silverfish can tolerate—and can withstand moderate humidity. It will be found around heating pipes and in similar situations in bakeries and kitchens.

Several years ago, specimens were sent to the Natural History Museum from a house in Galway, where the firebrat inhabited the airing cupboard in a house and also hid in the spaces between the floor tiles and walls of the kitchen. One was also recently found in a can of stout. Firebrats feed mainly on carbohydrates, substances which are plentiful in flour, crumbs and kitchen waste. The life-cycle, habits and development are similar to those of the silverfish.

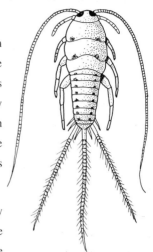

Firebrat –
Thermobia domestica
(Packard)

Cockroaches   Order: Blattodea

Common or Oriental Cockroach   *Blatta orientalis* Linnaeus

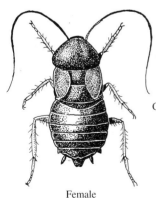

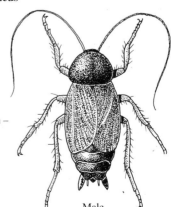

Common or Oriental Cockroach –
Blatta orientalis
Linnaeus

Female

Male

17

The common cockroach is large (17–30mm) and dark brown. The wings of the male are short and end well before the tip of the body. By contrast, those of the female are reduced to small flaps. The egg-cases contain an average of sixteen eggs.

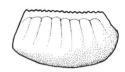

The commonest indoor cockroach in Ireland, it has been recorded from most counties. Being a versatile species, it occurs in a wide variety of buildings with artificial heating including factories, warehouses, hotels, hospitals, schools, restaurants and private

Egg-case

homes. The ideal conditions consist of a warm, damp environment with a plentiful food supply. Although unable to fly, it is very active and can move rapidly on smooth, vertical surfaces like walls.

German Cockroach *Blattella germanica* (Linnaeus)

This insect has a pale yellowish brown body, with two dark stripes on the thorax. It is one of the smaller species, reaching 10–15mm. Unlike the other cockroaches found in Ireland, the female carries the egg-case protruding from her body until the eggs are almost ready to hatch. During her life-time of several months, she will produce three to seven such cases, yielding thirty to forty-five nymphs each.

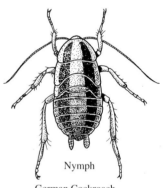

Nymph

German Cockroach –
Blattella germanica
(Linnaeus)

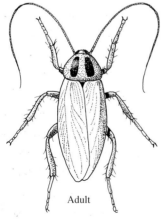

Adult

German Cockroach –
Blattella germanica
(Linnaeus)

The second commonest species, it has a variety of habitats ranging from homes to restaurants. Infestations also occur in hospitals, and specimens have even been discovered in sealed throat swabs. It prefers more heated conditions such as kitchens, bakeries and heating pipes, resulting in another popular name—'steamfly'.

Several years ago, the German cockroach caused an unusual incident at an Irish airport. When a leased aircraft returning from African service was fumigated, hundreds of cockroaches were killed hiding in such places as the drop-down oxygen masks for the passengers. What consternation and panic would have been unleashed if these cockroaches had poured out of the masks during a mid-flight emergency!

Brown-Banded Cockroach   *Supella longipalpa* (Fabricius)

Specimens are pale yellow or reddish brown, with brown cross-banding on the body. The body length of the adult varies from 10 to 14mm. During her lifetime, a female can produce ten to thirty egg-cases each containing on average eighteen eggs. The brown-banded cockroach is the most recent alien cockroach to form breeding colonies in Britain and Ireland and it can be a serious health hazard. In Ireland, the species was first reported from a Dublin flat in 1971 and there have been several subsequent records from the same city. Dead individuals have also been imported into Ireland behind a label on an Indian cane-work chair.

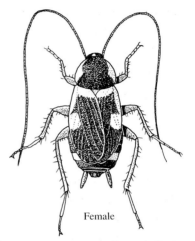

Female

Brown-Banded Cockroach –
Supella longipalpa
(Fabricius)

It has turned up in the residential buildings of two hospitals in Northern Ireland. In one of these, there was a heavy and active infestation which had been introduced in the personal effects of one of the doctors. All stages of the life-cycle were evident and numerous egg-cases were attached behind furnishings and high on walls.

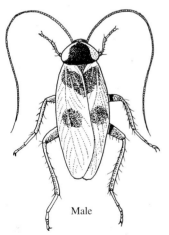

Male

Brown-Banded Cockroach –
Supella longipalpa
(Fabricius)

The brown-banded cockroach will be a serious pest if it becomes established in Irish hospitals. Unlike the German cockroach, which it resembles, it spreads throughout infested buildings. It prefers locations high in heated rooms and will also live in desk and bureau drawers, behind pictures, on book shelves where it feeds on the gum-bindings of books, behind wall paper where it feeds on paste, beneath tables and other furniture. It has a preference for lurking in furniture, bedding, cupboards and behind picture moulding and seldom visits kitchens except in search of food. This ability to disperse widely makes its control very difficult. Abroad, it has caused problems in hospital wards by emerging at night to feed on the body fluids of the

19

patients, often travelling from one person to another, and possibly causing the spread of infections and disease.

Australian Cockroach *Periplaneta australasiae* **(Fabricius)**

This large reddish or dark brown species grows to a length of 27–34mm when mature. The pronotum has a distinctive yellow submarginal ring. There are short yellow stripes on the front edges of the wings. The egg-case contains an average of twenty to twenty-six eggs.

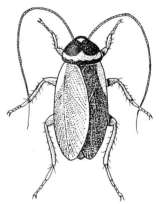

Australian Cockroach –
Periplaneta australasiae
(Fabricius)

The Australian cockroach is not a very common or well-established species in Ireland and it is most frequently encountered in imported produce (such as bananas from Ecuador, hardwood timber from Malaysia). The earliest record in these islands was from Belfast in 1887, but most Irish specimens have been found in Dublin, where it has continued to thrive in the National Botanic Gardens. Adults occurred in a storehouse in Offaly. In Britain, breeding colonies have been found in horticultural glasshouse nurseries, as well as in warehouses and other heated buildings.

American Cockroach *Periplaneta americana* **(Linnaeus)**

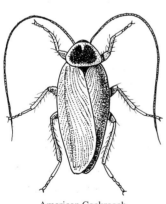

American Cockroach –
Periplaneta americana
(Linnaeus)

Another large (27–43mm) reddish brown species, resembling the Australian cockroach but lacking the stripes on the wings. A female may produce fifty or more egg-cases in her lifetime, containing on average fourteen eggs. An adult can survive for several months.

This species is voracious but is capable of surviving for long periods without food. It requires a higher mean temperature than the common cockroach. Abroad, it inhabits warehouses, hotels, schools, zoological gardens, bakeries, greenhouses, coal-mines and occasionally private houses. Like the Australian cockroach, it is not a common Irish species and is usually seen in imported goods (for example, in a crate from

Japan, rubber from Malaysia, bananas from Columbia, newspapers from India). In Offaly, when numerous adults and nymphs were discovered in a container of cotton from West Africa, the workers panicked and refused to work until the infestation was eliminated. It was common at one stage in a Dublin soap-factory, where the animal fat used to manufacture the soap provided it with a food source. It is not in fact dangerous.

Crickets and Grasshoppers   Order: Orthoptera

House Cricket   *Acheta domestica* (**Linnaeus**)

This species is a medium-sized (14–20mm) cricket with two pairs of wings (9–12mm long). It is greyish brown, with darker brown markings on the head and pronotum. The female has a long tube (ovipositor) for egg-laying. Long thread-like antennae are present and the hind legs are greatly enlarged and modified for jumping. However, specimens tend to run rather than jump except when alarmed.

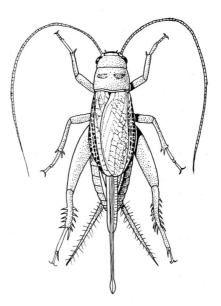

The eggs are small (2.5mm), white and cylindrical. At c. 20°C, they hatch in two or three weeks. There are usually eleven nymphal stages, taking from three to eight months to reach maturity. Active at night, crickets will eat a wide variety of foods, especially soft ones, including vegetables (cooked or uncooked), bread, dough, meat (raw or cooked) and even insects (alive or dead).

House Cricket –
Acheta domestica
(Linnaeus)
Female

The house cricket possibly arrived in these islands with returning crusaders in the thirteenth century. They were once common in Irish homes, occurring around the open hearth where many families kept a fire going for most of the day for cooking and warmth. Some people welcomed the cricket as a friendly guest because the song of the male was attractive—in his search for a mate, he can sing for hours at a time. In ancient China the singing was so highly esteemed that ladies of the

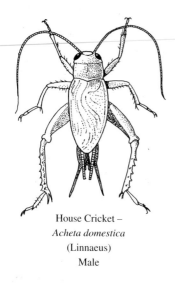

House Cricket –
Acheta domestica
(Linnaeus)
Male

imperial court kept the insects in gold cages close to their beds so that they could fall asleep to their song.

House crickets are generally harmless—though they occasionally gnaw small holes in various fabrics (such as woollens, cotton, silk), but unless there are large numbers present, the damage is usually very slight or barely noticeable. If you are lucky enough to have them in your home, do treasure them. Sadly, improved standards of domestic hygiene are gradually ousting this long-established species. For over thirty years, there was no confirmed record of the species in Ireland – the last one had been in 1960 – and some entomologists thought that the house cricket was extinct here. In 1991, however, it was discovered in a house in Castleknock, Co Dublin, when a female jumped out of a fireplace. Happily, the owners were delighted to conserve the colony.

Sometimes, faults in heating systems can make cricket-like sounds, resulting in erroneous reports.

The Greenhouse Camel-Cricket   *Tachycines asynamorus* Adelung

A medium-sized (11–15mm) insect with dark brown patterns on a lighter background, the species is wingless and has very long antennae and legs. Adults and nymphs are active at night and extremely difficult to catch.

In 1937, the first Irish specimen was discovered in a Dublin firm manufacturing minerals and aerated water but the first published record was only in 1976. A breeding colony was found under an animal cage in Dublin Zoo and had been in existence there for several years. Both adults

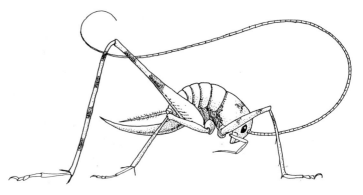

Greenhouse Camel-Cricket – *Tachycines asynamorus* Adelung

and nymphs lived in a three-foot gap transversed by hot-water pipes beneath a wooden cage floor and a concrete underfloor. A live specimen was collected in the tamarin monkey house in the Zoo in 1995. The species is mainly carnivorous, normally eating other insect pests, but it is suspected of damaging young plants. It could become a pest in heated greenhouses where valuable plants are grown, but it is unlikely to be encountered by householders.

Egyptian Grasshopper   *Anacridium aegyptium* (**Linnaeus**)

This large (50–80mm) brownish species is sometimes imported with vegetables, fruit or other

produce from the Mediterranean region, especially Italy. It is often erroneously mistaken for a locust but has distinctive dark patches on the hind wings. A harmless insect, it can be kept as a pet and fed on lettuce and similar foods.

Egyptian Grasshopper – *Anacridium aegyptium* (Linnaeus)

Earwigs   Order: Dermaptera

There are two native earwigs in Ireland, the common earwig (*Forficula auricularia* Linnaeus) and the lesser earwig (*Labia minor* Linnaeus). Only the common earwig causes problems indoors.

Common Earwig   *Forficula auricularia* Linnaeus

This insect is familiar to most people. Dark brown in colour, it has a distinctive shape with the body ending in large forceps or pincers. Adults range from 12 to 20mm and have two pairs of wings. The first set are scale-like, protecting the hind membranous ones, which can be used for flying. Strangely, specimens seldom do seem to fly.

Outdoors, they are abundant and widespread in Ireland, most gardens providing suitable habitats. They are omnivorous, feeding on a very wide range of foods. The female cares for her brood and both defends and feeds the young nymphs.

Common Earwig – *Forficula auricularia* Linnaeus

Frequently, earwigs wander accidentally into houses, factories and other buildings, often climbing up a drain pipe from a sink or bath. Active at night, when the dawn arrives they will seek out places to hide away from the light. They feel most secure in restricted places or crevices where both their upper and lower body surfaces are pressed against the walls of the hiding place. As a result, they may be found in books, towels or door jambs. In kitchens, they will often hide away in cooking utensils such as kettles and pots. This behaviour has resulted in dead earwigs being discovered in cups or pots of tea or coffee, in cooked meals or swimming in saucepans of porridge. Sometimes the manufacturer of the food product is erroneously blamed for the contamination.

Earwigs can be carried indoors in newly cut flowers (hiding among the petals), on clothes from the clothesline, in toys from the garden and so on. At night, they may wander considerable distances and end up in unusual places, especially within shops and factories. They occur frequently, but are not really a problem, except that people don't like them.

Booklice   Order: Psocoptera

Booklice are minute (1–3mm) insects, usually dark brown, whitish, yellowish or greyish in colour. They may be winged or wingless but most indoor species either have no wings or have very reduced unnoticeable wings. Because booklice are so small, most people find it difficult to identify them as insects with the naked eye and instead mistake them for mites. In some species there are both males and females but others can reproduce without males (parthenogenesis). The egg is huge in relation to the insect itself—about one-third the length of the adult. The young resemble the adults.

Popularly known as booklice, psocids or barklice, they are not related to the true lice. The similarity in some of the names of these two insect groups has caused confusion among the general public, however, and has even resulted in litigation. Psocids do not bite humans and their food consists of the microscopic moulds which grow in moist conditions.

Because of our damp climate, psocids are widespread in

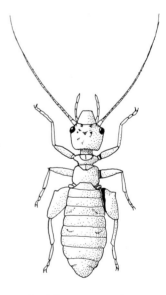

Book Louse – Psocoptera

Ireland and the domestic species probably occur in every house, often in the kitchen, in cupboards and larders. Fortunately, most householders are unaware of these co-habitors and if noticed, they are usually perceived as small dots moving actively about.

One species can draw attention to itself by making a tapping noise and it has been mistaken for the death-watch beetle in this country. There are many different species associated with stored, dry food products (such as flour, tea, cereals, dried pasta, sugar, corn flakes) which have become damp. A black species (*Lepinotus patruelis* Pearman) and a white one (*Liposcelis paetulus* Pearman) are among the commonest here.

In general, all the indoor species have similar requirements and behaviour. They love dampish conditions and prefer high humidity levels (75% or over). They can be numerous in places with condensation, ill-ventilated damp areas or new houses in which the plaster is still drying out. They have been found living in the debris between floorboards.

They are often associated with books and papers, especially when damp, and can cause damage by grazing on the minute fungal moulds, glues and pastes. They are virtually harmless in small numbers and in houses; they normally only cause problems when they enter foods which have not been kept sealed or stored in suitable conditions or have gone mouldy. Many shopkeepers and manufacturers have been unfairly blamed by irate customers for contaminated products when in reality the infestation originated in their own homes.

However, they can cause problems in flour mills and some consumer complaints may have a valid basis. In one grain silo in Northern Ireland, they became sufficiently numerous to cause complaints from the staff of the granary. They are a common pest in food stores or factories while problems of contamination can be caused in the pharmaceutical, medical and other industries where high standards of hygiene and cleanliness are required.

Psocids are difficult to identify and an experienced entomologist should be consulted for positive identifications. One exotic species (*Badonnelia titei* Pearman) has recently arrived in Ireland and is expected to become fairly widespread. Originally discovered on the back-binding of an atlas in England, it has now spread throughout Britain occurring in such places as clothes-drying cupboards. In Ireland, it infested a university library and the authors witnessed its arrival elsewhere in a consignment of books—on insects, as it happens—from Britain, which is perhaps a common means of dispersal.

Lice   Order: Phthiraptera

The true lice are divided into two major groups—biting (such as the dog-biting louse) and sucking lice (like the head, body and crab louse). Fortunately, biting lice seldom occur on people in Ireland and the sucking lice are the only species important for human health.

People can experience great discomfort caused by these insects—itchy heads, discomfort of the body or unbearable irritation in the groin.

Dog-Biting Louse   *Trichodectes canis* (De Geer)

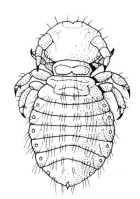

Dog-Biting Louse –
Trichodectes canis
(De Geer)

Superficially resembling booklice (page 24), the biting lice can be distinguished by their short antennae, body shape and prothorax. Most biting lice are external parasites associated with birds, and these species may accidentally enter houses from outdoor nests, but soon die without their hosts.

As its name suggests, the dog-biting louse is a parasite of dogs, which could occur indoors. It is a small (1.5mm) brown insect, flattened from top to bottom. A rare Irish species, there are only two old records (1938 and 1940) of this pest, both from Dublin. One specimen was found on a Kerry blue, while the other was on a six month-old pup.

Head and Body Louse   *Pediculus* spp

Two forms of the human louse are recognised, depending on whether they infest the head or body. In general, the two races keep very much to their respective parts of our bodies. The body louse is the larger and more robust of the two.

All the sturdy legs of both lice are about the same length, ending in hinged claws used for gripping hair. The abdomen is twice as long as it is broad. The adults are small (2–4mm) greyish wingless insects with their mouthparts adapted for piercing human skin and sucking blood. They may be distinguished from the unrelated booklice by their short antennae and from the biting lice by their fused thoracic segments.

The pearly oval eggs, popularly known as nits, are cemented to hair or clothing. There are three nymphal moults and all stages, including the adults, feed on human blood.

These insects have been responsible for great human suffering, not only causing discomfort but also diseases such as pediculosis (irritation of the skin), louse-borne relapsing fever and louse-borne typhus. By scratching themselves, people may open skin lesions and may introduce secondary infections such as impetigo.

Not only are they able to survive in close contact with man, but they are well adapted to evade his attentions. The force needed to burst (pop) a louse is about 500,000 times its own weight. (Don't try this: it can spread disease.)

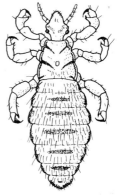

Head Louse –
Pediculus humanus
var. *capitis*
De Geer
Adult

The head louse (*Pediculus humanus* var. *capitis* De Geer) has been with us for a long time and specimens have been found on American Indian mummies several thousand years old. The female glues the nits or eggs one by one to individual hairs close to the scalp. As the hair grows, the nits are carried further out and become white or grey in colour when they hatch out. A female can lay eggs for up to twenty-eight days at the rate of eight or ten each twenty-four hours.

People who have had head lice for some time may begin to feel unwell due to irritation and sleeplessness. Children who have persistent nits do less well at school—hence the word 'nit-wit', often shortened to 'nit', for a stupid person.

Due to successful treatments of head lice in Ireland in the recent past, some people thought that these insects had disappeared for good. However, they are again a common problem. There are epidemics regularly, especially in schools. Although parents are not immune, they are affected less frequently than children.

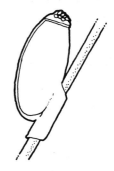

Head Louse –
Pediculus humanus
var. *capitis*
De Geer
Egg or Nit on hair

Unfortunately, some parents do not recognise infestations and are unaware of the preventative procedures (see Chapter 8). False pride can continue to allow this pest to thrive. The presence of head lice should not be considered a social disgrace and other parents should be informed of any infestations. A head-louse infestation does not indicate bad hygiene: in fact, these insects prefer clean, well-washed hair and do not like greasy, unwashed heads. If one individual in a school is infected, normal play contact (hair to hair) will be sufficient, unless the head lice are detected, for the rest of a group to become infected.

The body louse (*Pediculus humanus* var. *corporis* De Geer) is of major public health significance. This species has changed the course of human history by spreading diseases such as typhus and trench fever, resulting in the deaths of millions of people. It is not much of a problem where frequent washing and changing clothes is the rule, but infestation may be common where less attention is paid to hygiene.

Body lice lay their eggs for preference attached to garments, usually along the seams next to the skin. They hatch in some six days at body temperature. A single female can result in a colony of 15,000 viable females in eighty days, but the highest count has been 3800 specimens on one person.

If an individual has not been bitten previously, each bite produces a tiny spot that does not itch until after the first week, giving the lice ample time to lay eggs. In the second or third week, symptoms of sensitisation begin to appear and can be very irritating. The severity varies greatly between individuals, ranging from severe swelling to small red spots which hardly itch. Lice need to feed regularly every few hours. They can be transferred between humans through body contact.

Crab Louse *Pthirus pubis* (Linnaeus)

This insect may be distinguished from the head and body lice by its crab-like second and third pairs of legs. In addition, the abdomen is broader than it is long. The eggs are attached to hairs, the complete life-cycle taking twenty-five days.

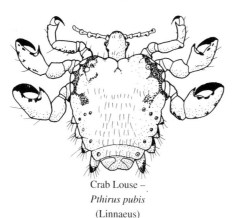

Crab Louse –
Pthirus pubis
(Linnaeus)

On our available information, the crab louse (also called the pubic louse) was only recently reported in Ireland and we know of only three records, all since the 1970s. Two of the patients had recently returned from holidays abroad. A very uncomfortable pest and probably widespread here, it may be under-recorded because infestations are usually associated with sexual activity. People normally become infected during sexual intercourse and the louse is popularly known as the 'butterfly of love' (*papillon d'amour*) in French.

Infestations can run in families and specimens can be passed from mothers to the eyelashes of their babies. Crab lice can occasionally be picked up from towels or from hairs with attached nits on toilet seats. Poor hygiene in cheap hotels can also result in infestations if clean bedclothes have not been provided between changes of guests. The crab louse normally inhabits the pubic area, grasping the coarse hairs with its claw-like legs. However, it can occur in beards, under the arms, on the eyelashes and sometimes on balding heads.

Since the louse is well-camouflaged and very small (1–2mm), it can be hard to find. But after feeding, specimens swell and become deep red. Heavy infestations can cause characteristic bluish spots around bite marks.

It is not known to transmit any disease. However, the bite is intensely irritating to the point of being almost unbearable. People who seek medical attention go to surgeries reduced to speechlessness and finger pointing. To avoid the embarrassment of a visit to the doctor, however, some infested people may resort to treating themselves by shaving the pubic area and destroying any suspect clothes or bedclothes to get rid of the infestation.

Thrips   Order: Thysanoptera

The name thrips is used, curiously, in both the singular and the plural.

These insects are very small (*c.* 1–7mm), mostly reddish or black, with a slender body and narrow wings fringed with hairs. They feed on vegetation, the mouth parts being adapted for piercing and sucking plant juices. However, they may bite humans causing severe discomfort. They are good fliers and when they get into the eyes or into clothing, they may cause considerable irritation.

After a series of relatively cool days in early summer, a rise in temperature can produce a

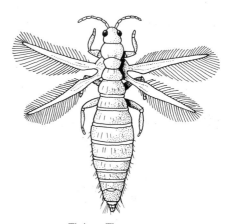

Thrips – Thysanoptera

29

mass flight of thrips, providing another common name—thunderflies. One of the thunderflies, *Limnothrips cerealium* Haliday, is sometimes abundant on cereal crops in Ireland.

When numerous, thrips may come indoors and create problems. This happened in Wicklow in October 1986, when specimens swarmed into a house and caused distress to the occupants by biting them. The dry climate of modern, centrally heated houses ensures that such interlopers will soon die off.

Thrips do occur as harmless contaminants of fresh vegetables, such as lettuce, but all that needs to be done is to wash the vegetables thoroughly to get rid of the insects. Manufacturers and retailers occasionally receive complaints from customers after finding thrips in the folds of packages or contaminating products.

In 1987, the western flower thrips (*Frankliniella occidentalis* (Pergandé)) was discovered in Dublin and Kerry. Subsequently, specimens turned up in Louth. This is a North American species now spreading throughout north-western Europe, being a notorious pest of many greenhouse crops including cucumbers, lettuce and chrysanthemums. It can be responsible for economic losses in greenhouses and it has proved difficult to control infestations despite frequent application of a combination of carbamate, organo-phosphate and synthetic pyrethroid insecticides.

Fleas   Order: Siphonaptera

Fleas are small (1–8mm) wingless insects with a complete metamorphosis or life-cycle (egg–larva–pupa–adult). In the adult, the body is flattened sideways and the colour varies from reddish brown to almost black. There are biting mouth parts.

A well-known feature is their jumping ability, used both for reaching their host and for escaping from danger. They are attracted to hosts by warmth and scent. The female must have a blood meal before she can lay fertile eggs — 448 have been counted from one individual flea.

The worm-like larvae are tiny (1.5–5mm), white and legless. They feed on organic debris in the sleeping places of their hosts and on partly digested blood in the excrement of the adults. The pupa is creamy–white later turning brownish. The newly formed adult inside the pupal skin or cocoon does not emerge immediately, but waits for vibrations caused by an arriving host.

A person's footsteps are sufficient to cause considerable numbers to emerge and seek their new host by jumping. This behaviour has resulted in large-scale flea attacks on people visiting abandoned or vacant houses. If this happens to you, consider stripping off your clothes in an empty bath, because the fleas will not be able to climb its smooth sides.

One such massive attack on a dog was witnessed in a holiday home in Clare some years ago. The bungalow had been empty for some weeks previously. The new visitors left the dog to sleep in the kitchen and were woken up in the early hours by piteous whining and howling. At first no problem could be seen but upon closer examination, hundreds of hungry fleas were seen crawling through the dog's coat. The dog suffered severe distress because of the intensity of the attack.

All adult fleas are parasitic on warm-blooded animals. Fortunately, most Irish species are harmless to humans, only attacking other mammals and birds. However, a small number can cause problems. An occasional bite may be a minor discomfort, but persistent attacks cause irritation and loss of sleep. People differ greatly in their reactions. Some are barely affected while others suffer from intense itching. In babies, scratching can lead to infections.

Fleas can also carry serious diseases, including plague and murine typhus. They may transmit dog tapeworms to humans if accidentally swallowed, which can happen with dead fleas in food or where people live in close contact with pets. The common pest fleas are described below and hints on their determination are included. However, the identification of fleas can be difficult and should be left to an entomologist if it is important to establish the identity of a species beyond question.

Human Flea *Pulex irritans* Linnaeus

The human flea is a small insect (2–3.5mm). Unlike the other fleas mentioned here, there are no oral or thoracic combs (spines) present in the adult and only one bristle on each side of the back of the head. As the name suggests, man is the main host but the species also occurs on pigs, dogs and other carnivores. The species will feed on pigs readily and will breed in profusion in pigsties.

In the past, the human flea was a familiar insect in Ireland and a preserved specimen was discovered during the excavations of Viking Dublin at Wood Quay. In the 1940s, specimens occurred on the back strand of the North Bull Island, Dublin, where thousands of bathers congregated during the summer months. Presumably, the fleas had hopped off discarded clothes and were waiting for new victims. Curiously, the species was once popular for use in flea-circus acts.

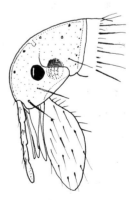

(Head of) Human Flea –
Pulex irritans
Linnaeus

Because of improvements in hygiene, especially the use of vacuum-cleaners which eliminates the young stages, they have now become rare in this country. Nowadays, the human flea is mostly associated with poor hygiene facilities, particularly among some vagrants and some refugees, but they can easily be picked up by other people.

The species prefers to infest and breed in bedrooms. They still occur in hotel rooms where they are carried accidentally by visitors.

The complete life-cycle may take only a month during summer but can vary depending on temperature.

Cat Flea   *Ctenocephalides felis* (Bouché)

The cat flea is another small insect (2–3.5mm). Both it and the dog flea have thoracic and genal combs. However, cat and dog fleas have differently shaped heads.

In general, cat fleas are found on cats (whereas dog fleas are found on dogs), but although the principal host of the cat flea in Europe is the domestic cat, there are records of the cat flea being found on dogs. Less commonly, the cat flea may attack rats, mice and other small mammals. It will bite man readily and viciously, often being the species responsible for infestations of fleas in houses in Britain.

(Head of) Cat Flea –
Ctenocephalides felis
(Bouché)

The species usually breeds where the cat sleeps but there may be other breeding sites such as armchairs. Indeed, the increased use of central heating and carpets has aided the spread of this pest, the eggs being deposited in the 'pile' of carpets, around skirting boards or in dusty inaccessible areas near the heating installations. Several persistent problems, where the affected people were mystified as to what was attacking them, were traced to cats which had gone wild. One of these involved large numbers of fleas attacking civil servants in a government department in Dublin where, due to the severity of the attacks, the staff threatened industrial action.

Dog Flea   *Ctenocephalides canis* (Curtis)

The principal hosts of this small flea (2–3.5mm) are the dog and the fox, although it can sometimes occur on cats. Where it does

(Head of) Dog Flea –
Ctenocephalides canis
(Curtis)

occur on cats, it is usually when the cats live in close association with dogs. The species can transmit a dog tapeworm (*Dipylidium caninum* (Linnaeus)).

In Ireland, the dog flea appears to be commoner than the cat flea—a reversal of the situation in Britain. It may become a pest in houses and will attack man without any reluctance.

European Chicken Flea *Ceratophyllus gallinae* (Schrank)

This flea ranges in size from 2 to 2.5mm. The thoracic comb is present but the genal one absent.

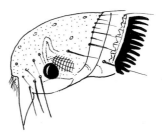

Also known as the hen-flea, this species is the commonest bird-flea in Ireland. It has been recorded from a great many different hosts, including both wild and domesticated birds. Large numbers of bird fleas can occur in abandoned birds' nests which are sometimes collected by children for school nature tables, etc.

(Head of) European Chicken Flea –
Ceratophyllus gallinae
(Schrank)

Infestations indoors often originate in the nests of starlings and sparrows. When the birds depart after nesting, hungry fleas may enter the house and attack the inhabitants, who may be badly bitten. One such incident in Donegal was traced to an abandoned nest in a chimney. Another infestation in Co Dublin had a more unusual source. House sparrows love to have dust baths which help them to get rid of their parasites. A woman became infested in her garden when she passed by one such bathing place and was attacked by the abandoned fleas. She was seriously affected by the bites (large bumps or blisters on the neck, face and other parts of the body).

Plague Flea *Xenopsylla cheopis* (Rothschild)

The plague or tropical rat flea varies from 1.5–2.5mm in length. Like the human flea, it lacks oral or thoracic combs, but has a row of bristles along the back of the head. This cosmopolitan species is the well-known carrier of bubonic plague. It occurs on rats that live in close association with humans, and also on various wild rodents.

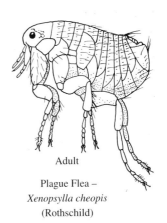

Adult

The plague flea is carried all over the world by ships' rats but is generally unable to maintain itself in these islands. In

Plague Flea –
Xenopsylla cheopis
(Rothschild)

Britain, it is mainly restricted to rat-infested areas near large sea-ports, where it lives on its normal host, the black rat, but it was found recently on brown rats in the underground part of Guy's Hospital, London, some distance inland. Central heating there provided favourable conditions for the flea to breed. In Ireland, we only know of one recent record. In 1976, Dr G. A. Walton discovered specimens on the body of a black rat from a flour mill in Cork city. (A history of the plague in Ireland is given in Chapter 9.)

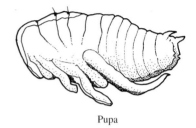

Pupa

Larva

Egg

Plague Flea –
Xenopsylla cheopis
(Rothschild)

Lacewings   Order: Neuroptera

Green Lacewing   *Chrysopa (Chrysoperla) carnea* Stephens

The adults are medium-sized insects (10–13mm), with the wings and body coloured a beautiful green, while the large eyes are sometimes a shining bronze. The two pairs of delicate, transparent wings are held tent-like over the body.

The species is widely distributed in Ireland but less frequently where there are no trees. Both the larvae and the adults feed on other insects. Because of the large numbers of greenfly that they consume, lacewings are very beneficial insects.

There are records of the adults from almost every week in the year, and during the autumn and winter months they may enter houses to hibernate. Specimens can be also attracted indoors by lights. They may be noticed resting on ceilings in rooms. If the temperature remains low, the overwintering lacewings will remain motionless, only waking up when the weather becomes warmer. However, if their hiding place becomes warm during the winter, they may wake too soon and then quickly die of hunger or thirst.

Green Lacewing –
Chrysopa (Chrysoperla) carnea
Stephens

Green lacewings are completely harmless to humans and they should never be killed. In spring, if you find adults alive in the house, open the window and let them fly out into the garden where they can once again search out and destroy greenfly. If they wake during the winter, place them in a cool place such as a loft or an outbuilding.

Chapter 3: True Bugs—Order: Hemiptera

On the Bed Bug

By day it lurks,

like a robber in the most secret part of the bed;

takes advantage of every chink and cranny,

to make a secure lodgement,

and contrives its habitation with so much art,

that scarcely any industry can discover its retreat.

Anon[4]

In North America, all insects are referred to as bugs, but true bugs are a group of insects that have powerful piercing mouthparts (proboscis). Since most are plant feeders, these are normally used to suck juices from stems, leaves and other parts, but some species can pierce human skin if they are mishandled. However, other bugs live on blood and will deliberately attack humans. The bed bug is the most important insect of this group in Ireland.

Cimicids   Family: Cimicidae

Bed Bug *Cimex lectularius* Linnaeus

The bed bug is one of the most unpleasant household pests in this country.

4 Quoted from The Natural History of Remarkable Insects with their habits and instincts, William de Veaux, Dublin, 1819 (probably edited by Rev. Charles Bardin)

Although it has small wing-pads, the adult bed bug is unable to fly. It reaches some 6mm in length and 3mm in width. Because of its mahogany brown colour and flat, saucer-like shape, this is a very distinctive-looking insect. There is also a pungent, sickly–sweet odour where it lives. The head is small, bearing a pair of long antennae. The proboscis, on the underside of the head, is

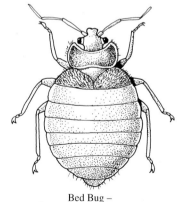

Bed Bug –
Cimex lectularius
Linnaeus

adapted for piercing human skin and sucking up blood. Since they have well-developed legs, bed bugs can walk quickly and climb up rough, vertical surfaces. The immature stages look like miniature adults but lack any wing-pads.

After feeding and mating, the female lays two or three eggs per day, totalling several hundred during her lifetime. The eggs are elongated (1mm), opaque and pearly white in colour. They are firmly glued to rough surfaces in crevices and cracks in walls and woodwork, behind wallpaper and in similar places.

The hatching nymph is only the size of an ordinary pinhead and is pale yellow. It can live for three or four months at low temperatures without food, but in order to moult and grow, it must have a blood meal. Before becoming adult, it will moult five times, growing and becoming darker in colour. All stages vary considerably in size, especially after a full blood meal, when the body swells up. Besides humans, bed bugs will attack animals such as birds, rodents and domestic pets.

Temperature and the availability of blood are the most important factors affecting development. At moderate room temperatures (18–20°C), the adults feed about once a week, but at 27°C about every three or four days. Adults in particular can withstand starvation for long periods, as long as a year at 13°C. At temperatures of 13°C or below, development is retarded and egg-laying, feeding and moulting stop. Feeding and breeding can occur throughout the year in those rooms where the temperature is always higher than 13°C. At 18°C, bed bugs normally live for a period of nine to eighteen months, but at higher temperatures their life span becomes progressively shorter—for example, about 10 weeks at 34°C.

Because of the successful use of insecticides, many people are now unfamiliar with bed bugs. Indeed, some health inspectors have mistaken them for beetles. As this pest has developed resistance to many of the commonly used insecticides, it is becoming widespread. Recent Irish records include top-grade hotels as well as ordinary houses.

Bed bugs are most adaptable creatures, experts at transferring from one building to another in second-hand and antique furniture, suitcases, removal vans and so on. There is an instance of a bed bug being observed crawling about on the fur coat of an old lady in church, although they do not normally travel on the body or clothing. One irate Leitrim landlady who wrote to the Natural History Museum suspected that the specimens she found in bed clothes had been introduced by two visitors 'of the long-haired type', who were staying on a fishing holiday. In fact, individuals can hide away in very narrow (1–2mm) crevices. During daylight, they are most successful in remaining unnoticed in cracks in walls, in nail or screw holes, behind skirting boards, peeling wallpaper or the backing of pictures. In one Irish infestation, over forty specimens were discovered hiding in the headboards of the victim's bed.

Although the bed bug has been blamed for spreading disease, there is little conclusive evidence to substantiate these claims. However, it is a regular feeder at night and repeated bites over a period of time will result in sleepless nights and lethargy for the victim. In addition, allergic reactions may be caused by injected saliva. The bites occur on those body parts most frequently exposed at night such as the shoulders and back.

A single bed bug can imbibe two to six times its own weight in blood in a visit, taking five to ten minutes to complete the meal. The species is most active just before dawn and is very skilful at finding victims. Bed bugs are often mysterious attackers, the only evidence of a visitation being bite marks and blood stains on the sheets: by the time the victim has awoken, the bed bugs are usually back in their hiding place.

Common Flower Bug *Anthocoris nemorum* **(Linnaeus)**

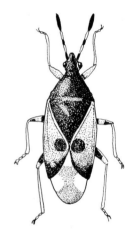

These small (4mm) insects, which are related to bed bugs, have a black body with brown-, yellow- and white-marked wings. The legs are yellowish brown. They live on other small creatures, sucking out their body fluids. As their prey includes greenfly and red spider mites, flower bugs are beneficial to gardeners. The species commonly occurs on woody plants and herbaceous plants. Adults are active from spring through to autumn but are most abundant during the summer months. Sometimes, they are accidentally brought indoors on fruit or on cut flowers. The long, thin proboscis, used to suck insect body fluids, can also draw blood, and if handled roughly, these insects can give a painful bite.

Common Flower Bug –
Anthocoris nemorum
(Linnaeus)

Shield Bugs or Stink Bugs   Family: Acanthosomidae

Although generally harmless, shield bugs sometimes cause alarm when noticed indoors. Like flower bugs, if roughly handled, they can give a nasty bite. In addition, a horrible smell may be produced, which is caused by a chemical secretion from glands on the underside of the body.

Hawthorn Shield Bug   *Acanthosoma haemorrhoidale*
(Linnaeus)

This is a large insect (15–16mm), predominantly green, with reddish areas. As the common name suggests, it feeds mainly on hawthorn and occurs outdoors in gardens and parks in urban areas from April to September. During the autumn, while looking for suitable hibernation sites, individuals may accidentally enter houses. There are also occasional records of shoppers finding them in purchased fresh fruit and vegetables.

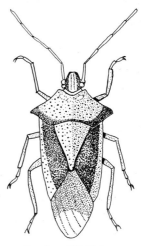

Hawthorn Shield Bug –
Acanthosoma haemorrhoidale
(Linnaeus)

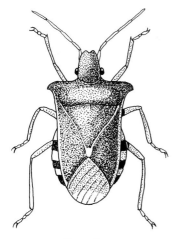

Forest Bug –
Pentatoma rufipes
(Linnaeus)

Forest Bug   *Pentatoma rufipes* **(Linnaeus)**

The forest bug (12–13mm) is very distinctive with its rounded, shoulder-like projections on the thorax. The species is dark brown and has an obvious red spot in the centre of the body. There are reddish markings along the sides. This shield bug feeds on sap and insects in woodland and orchards (especially apple, pear, cherry and hazel). Adults occur from July to November and are sometimes brought into the house accidentally on fruit. Like all insects in this group, they may sometimes bite.

Aphids—Greenfly or Blackfly   Family: Aphididae

Aphids are small (1–5mm) soft-bodied insects. The commonest are green but they may also be white, black and various shades of yellow, orange, red, brown or blue. The legs and antennae are relatively long, while the body ends in two conspicuous tube-like structures (siphunculi). Specimens can be winged or wingless. When there are wings, there are two pairs, which are broad and transparent.

These insects live on sap, using their syringe-like proboscis to pierce plants. Excess water and sugars ingested during feeding are excreted as sticky droplets called honeydew. Many ants and other insects eat this energy-rich substance, even 'farming' the aphids to obtain it.

Most aphids are females, capable of parthenogenesis—reproduction without males. When conditions are suitable, enormous numbers can be produced. With an ample food supply and no predators or disease, a single individual could give rise to ten million tons of offspring after only a hundred days of ideal weather conditions.

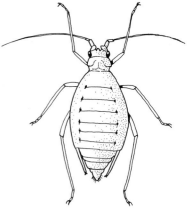

Wingless Greenfly –
Aphididae

Aphids may sometimes be found on lettuces, sprouts, cabbage or other vegetables, but are easily eliminated by washing thoroughly. There are no known health implications, but if a specimen is found in a salad sandwich, for example, this does indicate poor standards of hygiene in the preparation of the food.

A more serious aphid problem indoors is that some species can damage house plants. Black fungi may also grow on the

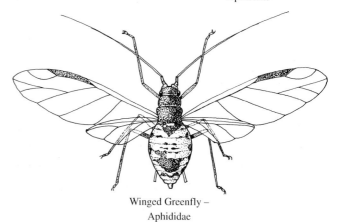

Winged Greenfly –
Aphididae

honeydew, causing a condition called sooty mould. This reduces the amount of light and air reaching the foliage, but it can be removed with a soft, damp cloth.

Already, two hundred species of aphid are known from Ireland and many more undoubtedly await discovery. Some are restricted to a particular plant, while others are general feeders.

Peach Potato Aphid   *Myzus persicae* (Sulzer)

Although usually various shades of green, this insect may also be pink, red or magenta. The size varies from 1.2 to 2.3mm. The peach potato aphid attacks hundreds of different plant species, including many economically important crops. It can also spread over a hundred different plant viral diseases. Asparagus, cabbage, celery, chicory, lettuce, parsley, spinach and watercress are among the affected vegetables and herbs.

Black Bean Aphid   *Aphis fabae* Scopoli

A matt black insect, 1.3–3.1mm long, which occurs on a wide variety of crops, such as beans (broad, French and runner), globe artichoke, lettuce, parsley, potato, rhubarb, spinach and tomato. It can spread over thirty plant viral diseases. A single generation can be completed in one week under favourable weather conditions.

Whiteflies   Family: Aleyrodidae

Adult whiteflies are delicate and small (2mm) insects, completely covered in a coating of white wax. They have two pairs of wings and resemble small moths. Most are white but dark or mottled forms do occur. The immature stages are oval and scale-like with radiating, tentacle-like filaments. They can easily be mistaken for scale insects. Like aphids, they excrete honeydew, which can result in sooty mould.

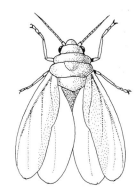

Whitefly –
Aleyrodidae
Adult

Whiteflies are a notorious indoor pest and occasionally occur outdoors. They are not a health hazard, but can cause serious damage to plants, about which the slowly flying adults may be noticed. Nineteen species are recorded from Britain and Ireland. Exotic species, which rarely survive for very long, are occasionally imported.

Each female lays a few dozen eggs and in some species no males are known. The life-cycle differs from that of other bugs, in that a flat, oval nymph hatches from the egg and then, after the first moult, loses its legs and antennae. Becoming scale-like and motionless, it continues to feed on the host plant. A pupal stage follows, which only stops feeding when the adult structures form inside. At 21°C, the complete life-cycle takes some three weeks, and at 15°C, four weeks.

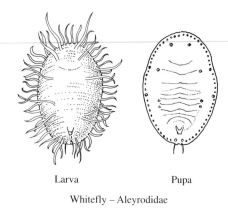

Larva   Pupa

Whitefly – Aleyrodidae

Glasshouse Whitefly   *Trialeurodes vaporariorum* (Westwood)

This whitefly is very common and a destructive pest on indoor plants, especially begonias. Originating in the tropics and sub-tropics, it was accidentally introduced into Ireland and is now widespread in glasshouses. Adults may live for over a month and each female can lay two hundred eggs on the underside of the leaves. The eggs hatch in about ten days and the immature stages feed for two weeks. The species can breed continuously.

Scale Insects and Mealy Bugs   Superfamily: Coccoidea

Scale insects and mealy bugs are normally small (up to 5mm).

Scale insects have no obvious body divisions or segmentation. With their reduced or absent legs, they appear as rather featureless white, yellow or brown, waxy, scale-like blemishes on indoor plants. They are covered with a hard or waxy scale. By contrast, the mealy bugs are protected by a mass of waxy threads. Adult males occur in some species of both scale insects and mealy bugs and they resemble very small flies.

The female and immature scale insects and mealy bugs sit motionless on the plant, feeding through a proboscis. They are amazingly prolific: a single female can lay a thousand eggs. Over six generations, she can give rise to over thirty million insects. Some species produce live young, which are usually protected in a variety of ways, under overlapping plates of wax or in or under the mother's body. The young then disperse over the plant searching for a suitable feeding site.

Honeydew and sooty mould are problems associated with these bugs.

Mussel Scale   *Lepidosaphes ulmi* (**Linnaeus**)

These insects resemble sea-shore mussels and occur especially on plant stems and branches. Cyclamen, geraniums, poinsettias are among the affected indoor plants, which may wilt if attacked by mussel scale.

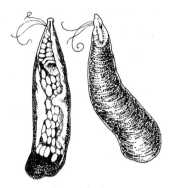

Mussel Scale –
Lepidosaphes ulmi
(Linnaeus)

Hemispherical Scale   *Saissetia coffeae* (**Walker**)

This species has red-brown convex shells and is found encrusting the stems and leaves of many plants. Although rarely reported in Ireland, we believe that it is widespread in heated conditions. It is very common in such situations in the National Botanic Gardens and the Dublin Zoological Gardens. It has also been observed in domestic houses.

Hemispherical Scale –
Saissetia coffeae
(Walker)

Soft Scale   *Coccus hesperidium* **Linnaeus**

Also occurring on a wide range of plants, soft scales have yellow-brown, flat, oval shells.

Mealy Bugs   *Pseudococcus* **spp**

These grey–white soft-bodied insects infest cacti, succulents, ferns and many other plants. They secrete white, waxy fibres that cover their colonies and egg masses. They live on relatively inaccessible parts of the plant.

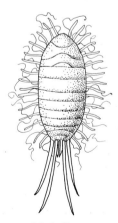

Mealy Bug –
Pseudococcus sp

Chapter 4: Beetles—Order: Coleoptera

Death-Watch Beetle

With teeth or with claw it will bite or will scratch,

And chambermaids christen this worm the death watch,

Because like a watch it always cries click;

And woe be to those in the house who are sick!

For sure as a gun, they will give up the ghost,

If the maggot cries click, when it scratches the post.

Dean Jonathan Swift

Beetles are among the most common and widespread of Irish insect pests. Adult beetles are usually sturdy and compact insects, with a hard 'skin'. In most groups the first pair of wings are hard, opaque and shell-like, which cover or nearly cover the abdomen from above. The second pair of wings (if present) are membranous and used for flying but when at rest these are folded and concealed under the shell-like first pair of wings.

Furniture and Related Beetles   Family: Anobiidae

Furniture Beetle (Woodworm)   *Anobium punctatum* **(De Geer)**

The female is larger than the male, but both are easily identifiable by the presence of a raised pronotum (front part of the thorax) when viewed from the side. They range from 2.5 to 5mm and are variable in colour, from light reddish yellow through dark chocolate to dark red.

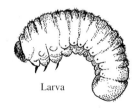

Larva

Furniture Beetle –
Anobium punctatum
(De Geer)

The furniture beetle is a very serious pest, causing damage costing millions of pounds annually in this country. In Britain, it is estimated that three-quarters of all buildings harbour this species, usually in the roof space. The young stages, or woodworm, attack wood, feeding inside and considerably weakening such load-bearing timbers as floorboards and roof joists. The characteristic circular emergence holes of the adults can disfigure both modern and antique furniture. Books may be also damaged. Furniture beetles prefer soft woods, especially plywood, but hardwoods are also attacked. Householders may be unaware of a serious infestation until the males are discovered on window sills. This can happen at any time of year, but there is a peak of activity in June and July in Ireland.

The species is very common in the wild, inhabiting the dead parts of living trees or where bark has been removed. Adults will readily enter premises during the summer months. In addition, they are spread in infested furniture by families moving home. The females are poor fliers, and mating can take place in their emergence holes.

Normally the female searches out uncured or badly cured softwood for egg-laying, but there are few timbers that are immune from attack. She particularly likes rough areas or where joints have opened. Even very expensive furniture may

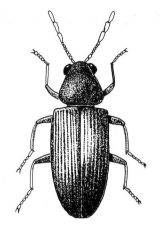

Adult

Furniture Beetle
Anobium punctatum
(De Geer)

Side View of Adult

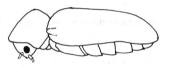

have parts made of softwood and these are always potential sources of infestation. After hatching from the white, lemon-shaped eggs, the small larvae bore into the timber. They are usually whitish with brown heads and have special bacteria in their guts which allow them to digest the cellulose in the wood. The life-cycle may take three years or longer.

Death-Watch Beetle   *Xestobium rufovillosum* (De Geer)

The adults are 5–7mm in length, dark chocolate brown with patches of yellowish hair. They have a characteristically widely flanged prothorax (front of thorax).

Like the furniture beetle, this beetle infests wood, but by contrast with it, this is a very rare Irish species and evidently our damp and cold climate does not suit it. Nevertheless, serious damage has been caused to several of our historical buildings including Leinster House, St Patrick's Cathedral, Rathfarnham Castle and the Royal Hospital. These infestations originated in old British oak imported for use as roof or structural timbers.

The larval stage may take ten to twelve years to mature, making detection more difficult, but under optimum conditions the entire life-cycle can be completed in twelve months. There have been cases abroad of infested cavities in large structural timbers, where the extent of the attack could not have been assessed from outside.

Both sexes make a characteristic tapping sound by knocking their heads against the wood on which they are standing. This behaviour has given rise to the popular name. In Ireland, one of the common booklice or psocids also makes a ticking sound and this is often responsible for householders fearing that they have an infestation of death-watch beetles. However, we have never encountered an infestation of these beetles in ordinary domestic premises.

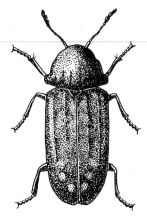

Death-Watch Beetle –
Xestobium rufovillosum
(De Geer)

Biscuit Beetle   *Stegobium paniceum* (Linnaeus)

The adults are small (2–4mm) reddish brown insects, which resemble furniture beetles. However, they lack the raised pronotum. In the past, the species was often abundant in biscuits on sailing ships—hence the popular name. The habit of banging these biscuits on a table before eating them was an attempt to get rid of the insects inside.

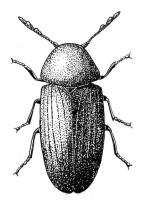

Biscuit Beetle –
Stegobium paniceum
(Linnaeus)

The biscuit beetle is found throughout the world, and is known in North America as the drugstore beetle. This is an amazingly adaptable creature, breeding in every conceivable type of vegetable and animal product, including the hottest spices. It can be a serious pest of preserved plants in herbaria, and it was discovered recently in Ireland eating ornamental flowers imported from the orient. The species may even live in poisonous substances such as belladonna, strychnine and aconite.

Indeed, this ability resulted in one Irish pest eradication firm inadvertently *causing* an infestation. The company placed trays containing poisoned wheat and rice throughout a public building in Dublin for rodent control. They were unaware that the baits were infested with biscuit beetles. The insects were unaffected by the poison and continued breeding. Within a short time, there were numerous complaints from the staff about strange beetles flying about everywhere and landing on the paperwork or in cups of coffee. The beetles were searching for new places to colonise and even occurred in a library containing very rare books. Despite the removal of the infected trays, it took a long time to eradicate all the biscuit beetles. A similar incident of beetles 'plaguing' workers in a post office probably had the same cause.

The biscuit beetle is one of the commonest and most economically important pests that attacks stored products, and its association with humans is known from as long ago as 2500 B.C. in Egypt. The diet includes cereals, beverage concentrates, herbs, animal foodstuffs, cocoa beans, liquorice, spices (even chilli peppers) and various drugs. The adult flies readily and, during an infestation, beetles are often first noticed crawling on windows. Specimens can be carried from building to building in and on goods or clothing. The adults do not feed but can eat their way through packaging in order to lay their eggs in a food source, and so infest the contained products.

A single adult female can lay about a hundred eggs either in the food itself or in crevices nearby. When newly hatched, the white larvae are only 0.5mm long and 0.12mm wide. As a result, they can squeeze through the narrowest cracks or penetrate the wrappings on food with relative ease. With their long legs and keen sense of smell, they are very agile and well equipped to search for food. Furthermore, they can survive for over a week without nourishment. At 22°C, the life-cycle takes two to three months. In heated buildings, adults can occur at any time of the year. As well as attacking foodstuffs, this species can cause structural and other damage in the last larval stage by creating a hollowed protective chamber in which to pupate, and materials which may be damaged include cardboard, books, wood and even sheet lead.

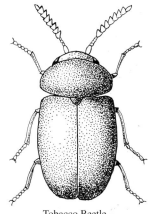

Tobacco Beetle   *Lasioderma serricorne* (Fabricius)

The adults are somewhat oval, small (2–4mm) and reddish brown with dense, short hairs. Their serrated antennae distinguish them from the furniture and biscuit beetles.

The tobacco beetle is primarily a tropical and subtropical species which requires plenty of warmth. In Ireland, it can only survive in heated buildings and is a very rare pest. It was first recorded here from tobacco leaf in 1932. Only the larval stage

Tobacco Beetle –
Lasioderma serricorne
(Fabricius)

feeds, and they can penetrate tiny holes in search of food. As the names suggests, this species can tolerate nicotine and is a serious pest of tobacco products. However it will also attack dried fish, cereals, cereal products, spices, pulses and other food of vegetable origin.

Spider Beetles   Family: Ptinidae

The common name is derived from the shape of the adult which, with its long legs and rounded body resembles a spider. There is a distinct division between the thorax and the arched abdomen. The larvae are white. Several species are pests in Ireland and they can occur together. The commoner spider beetles are described below, but others can occur.

Australian Spider Beetle   *Ptinus tectus* Boieldieu

The adults are small (2.5–4mm) and yellowish brown. As the common name indicates, this insect was first associated with Australian wheat and can be a serious pest in grain stores in Ireland. This species is a relatively recent arrival in this country and was first recorded in November 1907, when it was found in a tin of almonds in Killiney, Co Dublin. It is now a common and widespread indoor pest here. Infestations are often unnoticed, because the adults emerge at night and large numbers can easily be overlooked. Such problems may originate in bird and rodent nests, for the species will feed on dead and desiccated pigeons, rats or other dried animal remains. Food products can be infected from these sources by beetles following water pipes or electric cables from the attic to the basement or *vice versa*.

The female can lay up to a thousand eggs and large populations can quickly build up, the full life-cycle taking three to four months. The species is capable of surviving in even small amounts of mixed organic debris in deep cracks and crevices such as occur in warehouses. The newly hatched larvae are very agile but upon reaching a food source, they become inactive and grub-like. This is the most damaging stage and almost anything of animal or vegetable origin is eaten including flour, grain, spices, chocolate, nuts, dried fruit, cereal products, dried soup powder, animal faeces (rat, mouse and similar) and the remains of dead insects or other animals. When fully mature, the larva

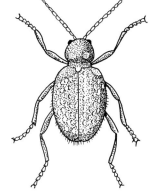

Australian Spider Beetle –
Ptinus tectus Boieldieu

seeks a pupation site and then it may cause damage to tougher materials such as sacking, cellophane, cardboard, books, wood and even lead. Textiles may be gnawed by both larvae and adults, producing small, regular, round holes.

In addition to its widespread occurrence in buildings, there are numerous fascinating Irish records of this pest. These are just a few of them: numerous adults in a bag of rayon cleaning buds purchased in a supermarket; in the plastic liners of assembled cardboard boxes; numerous larvae found on a plate containing ham and crispbread in a café (the crispbread was old stock); in spice in a Chinese restaurant; in the rice of a curry in another restaurant; adults feeding on dog-food stored in an attic; in the linings of disposable nappies; abundant in a box of dried fishfood (*Daphnia*) bought in an old shop; with furniture beetles in a roll of carpet purchased by a convent.

Two instances merit more detailed accounts. The Australian spider beetle almost jeopardised a large foreign order for Irish-made pharmaceutical products by contaminating tubes of antiseptic ointment. When the customers abroad opened the tubes to use the ointment, they discovered dead beetles on the inside of the lids—not a good recommendation for an antiseptic product! Such tubes are supplied to pharmaceutical companies with the lids already fitted and the bottoms left open for filling. Further investigation revealed that before they were filled, these tubes were stored in a warehouse, where they were stacked with the open end upright, acting as traps which captured wandering beetles at night. During filling, the antiseptic ointment then covered the trapped beetles. The problem was solved when the tubes were stored the other way around.

An excellent example of the adaptability of this insect involved newlyweds who, on moving into their new home, were astonished to discover large numbers of beetles wandering about, especially in the bedrooms. An intensive investigation of these rooms did not reveal any source for the infestation. Finally, the attic was checked and the problem was located there. Extraordinary in this day and age, the builders of the house had used the attic as a toilet and the beetles were breeding in the dried human excrement.

White-Marked Spider Beetle   *Ptinus fur* (Linnaeus)

This beetle is similar in size and colour to the Australian spider beetle but the adults normally have white patches of scales on the wing-cases. The males and females differ in form.

A cosmopolitan species, it was widespread at the turn of the century but in Ireland it occurred only locally, especially in Co Down, where it was plentiful in a few ancient warehouses, apparently living in debris in deep cracks. It also occurred in quantities in preserved goods.

In our experience, this is now a rare Irish species and we have received only one record in the last twenty years. An angler tying fishing flies in Leixlip, Co Kildare, discovered the species living within the shafts of birds' feathers, which he had purchased commercially in this country.

The female only lays fifty eggs. The larvae feed on a variety of dried and decaying vegetable and animal matter including offal, dead insects, wasp combs, stuffed birds, feathers, animal skins, dried plants, spices, dried fruit, flour, bakery products, grain and other stored cereals.

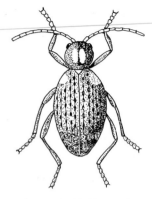

White-Marked Spider Beetle –
Ptinus fur (Linnaeus)

Golden Spider Beetle   *Niptus hololeucus* (Faldermann)

Another cosmopolitan species, this small (3–4mm) beetle is almost completely covered with small yellow scales and long outstanding hair. It is known to have been brought to Europe from Asia Minor in the middle of the nineteenth century in pigs' bristles and from southern Russia in rhubarb roots. It was once common in Irish houses but seems to have become scarcer, perhaps due to competition from the Australian spider beetle. However, large numbers infested a Dublin house in 1984, and it was abundant in the damp and mouldy basement of a bookshop in 1989. It can occur in older warehouses.

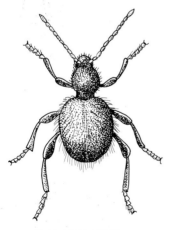

This insect is mainly a scavenger and is frequently found in association with rodent nests and droppings. It is not an important pest of stored food, but the larvae may damage spices, drugs, cereals and cereal products. Their diet also includes dead insects, rodent droppings, textiles, upholstered furniture, woollen blankets, books and papers stored for long periods, leather goods, cotton, linen and stored seed. They may be found amongst miscellaneous vegetable and animal debris in warehouses, poorly kept storerooms, cellars, old houses, flour mills and bakeries.

Golden Spider Beetle –
Niptus hololeucus
(Faldermann)

Globular Spider Beetle *Trigonogenius globulus* **Solier**

The small (2.5–3.5mm) adults are greyish in colour. Widely distributed in temperate regions, the species is rare in this country. The first Irish specimens were discovered in imported clover seeds in 1921, but there are few records. It has occurred in mills, grain stores and houses. Beetles were also found inhabiting beds in a public building, while the bedrooms were being prepared to receive foreign dignitaries. The species consumes a variety of dried animal and vegetable materials including animal hooves and horns, oilcake, cotton, flour, dried seeds and dried fruit.

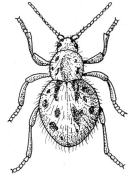

Globular Spider Beetle –
Trigonogenius globulus
Solier

Hide, Larder and Carpet Beetles   Family: Dermestidae

Varied Carpet Beetle *Anthrenus verbasci* **(Linnaeus)**

The adults are small (1.7–3.2mm), with a variegated pattern of golden yellow and black and white scales. A cosmopolitan species, it is a serious household pest in England especially in the south-east where it now surpasses the clothes moth in the amount of damage done to property. Indoors, it is best known for attacking woollen goods (carpets, bedclothes, clothing and so on), but it also eats the glue of book bindings. In addition, it is a serious pest of dried insect and mammal collections and is sometimes called the 'museum beetle'.

The species has been reported from numerous stored products including savoury biscuits, dried baby food, flour, peanuts, seeds, grain, rice, cacao, drugs, dried cheese, health food tablets, rusks and cayenne pepper. Infestations can originate from birds' nests or dead animals such as mice under floorboards, the larvae migrating towards a heat gradient and appearing in airing cupboards and under carpets. Electrical faults in a telephone exchange were caused when larvae ate the cotton/wool insulating material.

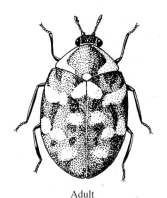

Adult

Varied Carpet Beetle –
Anthrenus verbasci
(Linnaeus)

Larva

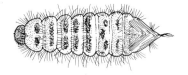

The larvae are brown, quite hairy and 4.0–5.0mm in length when mature. Known as 'woolly bears', they feed actively and then have a resting period, with successful development taking place between 15°C and 25°C. Indoors, the life-cycle can be completed within a year. When the adults emerge, they usually fly to the windows and eventually escape out of doors. They can live for between 13 and 44 days, facilitating their dispersal.

The varied carpet beetle appears to be a recent newcomer to this country and, if it successfully colonises Ireland, it will become a serious pest. In 1984, adults were noticed crawling on the window ledges of an upstairs bedroom in Ranelagh, Dublin. The source of this infestation was not found. Subsequently, another infestation was discovered in a flat off Pearse Street, Dublin. Larvae occurred there under carpeting and among floorboards.

Two-Spotted Carpet Beetle   *Attagenus pellio* (Linnaeus)

Also known as the fur beetle, the two-spotted carpet beetle is widely distributed but relatively rare in Ireland. Both the adults and the larvae are very distinctive in appearance, the former having two characteristic white spots on the wing covers and ranging in size from 3.5 to 6mm. Possessing a tuft of long hairs at the rear end, the larvae are popularly known as 'woolly bears'.

From March to September, the adults can be seen outdoors, where they feed on nectar and pollen. Under such wild conditions they lay their eggs in the nests of both mice and birds, the larvae feeding on hair, feathers and excrement. Most indoor infestations originate from such sources.

However, some are caused by the adults entering premises, since they can live for three months and are good fliers. Indoors, the larvae feed on animal products or materials including smoked meat and fish, furs, skins, woollens, carpets, upholstered furniture, bolting silk (that is, silk used for sifting flour) in flour mills and dried museum specimens, especially insects. Specimens can occur on grain or cereal products, but they may need the remains of other insects found in these products as supplementary food in order to survive. The life-cycle varies between six months and three years.

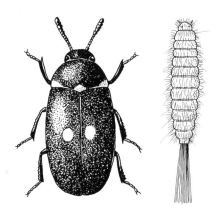

Adult   Larva

Two-Spotted Carpet Beetle –
Attagenus pellio
(Linnaeus)

In southern England, this beetle is a common pest and is of economic importance. In Ireland, it is only an occasional nuisance. At the turn of the century, it was associated with lumber rooms and stores. It has also been found in cellars and dark corners. More recent records include a carpet infestation in Thurles, Co Tipperary and an adult and larva discovered under linoleum in Dublin. The species has also been imported into this country in a shipment of cotton goods from North America.

Bacon Beetle *Dermestes lardarius* Linnaeus

Also called the larder beetle, this is another distinctive insect and is commoner than the two-spotted carpet beetle. The large adults (7–9.5mm) have characteristic markings, while the larvae are bristly and can grow to 10–17mm. There is usually one generation in a year. Both stages will feed on almost any animal substance which is dry or in the process of decomposition. The diet includes skins and furs, bones, bone and fish meal, horn and hooves, hair, leather, feathers, dried fish, cheese, bacon, ham, sausages and silkworms. They will occasionally feed on dry vegetable matter.

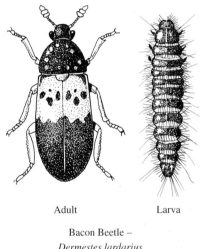

Adult   Larva

Bacon Beetle –
Dermestes lardarius
Linnaeus

The bacon beetle has been known to kill young pigeons, ducklings and chickens and in Britain it can be a pest in deep pit poultry houses. When fully grown, the larvae leave the food and during their search for a pupation site, they can damage and tunnel into almost any compact material including tobacco, cork, woollens, vegetable fibre, wood, lead, tin and even the mortar and stonework of walls.

Indoor infestations sometimes originate in nearby birds' nests but the adults fly well and may have come from far away. There are recent Irish records from houses, shops, restaurants, a bakery and a chocolate factory. Specimens were discovered in biscuits, cooked curry, flour and pupating in chocolate. In one instance, live larvae were found crawling on a chocolate bar which was submitted for examination after the consumer suffered from diarrhoea. Another infestation, in a flat, was traced to meat debris which was left behind a fridge by the previous tenants.

In the past, the bacon beetle was a commoner pest, but improvements in hygiene have reduced its numbers, the most important being the use of refrigerators and deep freezes for storing meat products. Being relatively large and slow-growing, it is vulnerable to control measures.

Related species are sometimes imported and in 1976, both adults and larvae of *Dermestes carnivorus* Fabricius were discovered in a parcel from Hong Kong. It contained dried fish bladders destined for a Chinese restaurant in Dublin city. The consignment was subsequently destroyed following court proceedings.

Khapra Beetle *Trogoderma granarium* Everts

The small (1.8–3mm) adults are elongate–oval in shape. They are brown to brownish black, with the body densely clothed in fine yellowish hairs. The larvae are also very hairy.

Abroad, the species is a serious pest of stored products especially grain. Large populations can arise in a very short space of time. Originating in India, it probably first arrived in Britain in 1917. Although once a serious pest in maltings and granaries there, it is now rarely found and may no longer be established.

There are few Irish records. In 1943, it was first reported from tea chests from India and was later found in a distillery silo. This had contained heated grain and the larvae lived in the crevices between the slats of the wooden bins. The infestation survived for about a year before dying out. In

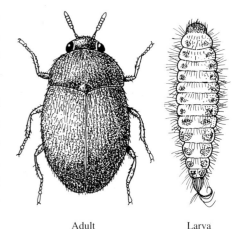

Adult   Larva

Khapra Beetle –
Trogoderma granarium
Everts

the 1940s, the species inhabited a flourmill silo and a provender mill in Belfast. In the 1970s, it was discovered in an oat storage bin in Northern Ireland. There are also records from Cork, Derry and Limerick. The species can only breed in heated conditions (21°C or more) and is unlikely ever to be a serious pest here.

Oedemerids   Family: Oedemeridae

Wharf Borer *Nacerdes melanura* **(Linnaeus)**

The large (7–14mm) adult is yellowish brown, covered in dense yellow hairs, and the wing-case tips are black. The wharf borer resembles the very common Irish soldier beetle (*Rhagonycha fulva* (Scopoli)) but has three longitudinal lines on the wing-cases while lacking the lateral flanges on the prothorax. In addition, there are only four tarsal segments in the hind leg compared with five in the soldier beetle. The mature larva is greyish white, slender and 12–30mm long. It has been described as resembling a string of beads.

Although believed to have originated in the Great Lakes area of North America, the species has now been carried to all parts of the temperate world by ships. As the name implies, it occurs in wharf timbers between flooding and the high-water level. Infestations are usually in softwoods but have been reported from damp or wet oak. Some habitats are unusual, such as the bases of telegraph posts wetted by dog urine and around the base of water closets.

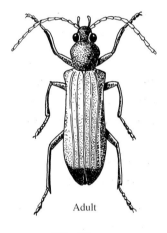

Adult

Wharf Borer –
Nacerdes melanura
(Linnaeus)

In Britain, there are inland occurrences, but despite being known from this country since 1854, there are surprisingly few Irish records. We are only aware of three recent ones and all are from the month of June when the adults were noticed. In Wexford town, large numbers of beetles infested a dwelling house. It is believed that they originated in the nearby wooden quays. Beetles were found to be abundant in two houses in Dublin, after specimens were sent to the Natural History Museum for identification. One, in Ringsend, was about a hundred years old with rising and penetrating damp. There was also unsatisfactory ventilation. A one-year-old suite of furniture and a new wall cabinet had been eaten by the larvae.

Larva

Mould Beetles   Families: Cryptophagidae and Lathridiidae

Also known as plaster beetles, these small (1–3mm) insects range in colour from pale brown to black. In the wild, they are very common, living on all kinds of fungi especially moulds. In both families, the antennae of the adults end in clubs. Among the common pest species, the cryptophagids have a central tooth on each side of the pronotum while the lathridiids have strong ridging or rows of pits or depressions on the wing-cases.

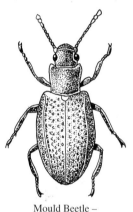

Mould Beetle –
Lathridius sp

Because of our wet climate, these insects are sometimes the bane of Irish householders, who may find the beetles crawling on walls and ceilings, often in large numbers. They are not harmful to human health, but, since they graze on moulds, mildews or other fungi, they are indicative of damp conditions. They may be numerous in new or recently renovated premises where fungi have developed due to the incomplete drying out of plaster or cement and high humidity. They also occur in old and neglected houses, especially in dank cellars or on walls where wallpaper is peeling off due to damp. Unpainted woodwork, with a high moisture content, may also attract these insects. An infestation can last several months in a new house until it is dried out with heat and good ventilation.

They also feed on damp stored products including cardboard. Some species can be prevalent in food factories, living on old mildewed goods, particularly when they have accumulated unnoticed behind wall panelling or in inaccessible parts of machinery. This problem is more severe where powdered foods are involved. Complaints may be received by such firms after specimens have wandered into fresh produce or food containers.

Other Irish records include adults in a warehouse in Cork city and numerous beetles in the packing room of laboratories in Co Mayo. After samples were sent to the Natural History Museum for analysis from Co Cork, all stages were found to be abundant in grain that had become mouldy in intervention stores.

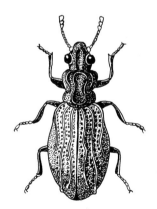

Mould Beetle –
Aridius nodifer
(Westwood)

In this country, the small (1.2–1.6mm) and distinctive species *Aridius nodifer* (Westwood) is the plaster beetle most frequently submitted for identification—it is conspicuous because of its black colour.

Weevils   Family: Curculionidae

The weevils are the most successful of all insects and over 50,000 species are now known. They all have a characteristic snout projecting from the head, though in a few this may be short. Only a few cause indoor problems in Ireland.

Vine Weevil   *Otiorhynchus sulcatus* (Fabricius)

This large (8–10.5mm) black beetle has patches of yellow and white scales on its wing-cases. The species is a serious horticultural and agricultural pest. It also attacks garden plants in glasshouses, houses and out of doors.

The females can reproduce without males, each laying as many as a thousand eggs in soil and potting media. As a result, a single specimen can start a serious infestation. The legless white larvae (up to 8mm) feed on the roots, corms and tubers of many plants. They can be very troublesome in pot- or container-grown plants in houses and greenhouses. At the least, the destruction of roots will check growth but the plant may also wilt and die. The adults feed at night on leaves and shoots, hiding away during day-light.

Vine Weevil –
Otiorhynchus sulcatus
(Fabricius)

Characteristic damage includes irregular holes or ring-barking. All stages may be killed with insecticides or during repotting. In addition, nematodes are now used to control this pest.

Irish householders are sometimes astonished to find the adults wandering about their premises. Because of their size, the discovery of these insects may cause anxiety that the house is being attacked by a super woodworm beetle. However, the answer is more prosaic and the occurrence is usually traceable to a recently purchased potted plant. Since it is a common pest in nurseries, many such plants are infected. When the flightless beetles emerge during darkness to feed, they may fall out of the pot. Unable to climb back up the smooth sides, they are then found on a window ledge or elsewhere in the room. They may be numerous and can wander some distance. In one Wicklow infestation, twelve adults were collected in one day from double glazing covering plants and from the dining room ceiling, stairs and walls.

Wood-Boring Weevils *Pentarthrum* **and** *Euophryum* **spp**

There are three species of these small beetles (2–5mm) and all are similar in appearance, their colour varying from blackish brown to reddish brown. These weevils originated in New Zealand and two occur in the wild in Ireland. Adults are reluctant to fly, and specimens occurring indoors are probably transported from one building to another on people's clothing or in goods. Outdoors, birds may carry the weevils from place to place.

Wood-boring weevils attack a variety of timbers that are already partially fungally decayed. Both hardwoods and softwoods are affected. In Britain, they commonly infest panelling in damp situations. Damp flooring blocks have also been infected. It was once thought that small patches of wet rot in premises were of no significance if allowed to dry out. However, this is no longer the case wherever these weevils occur.

Wood-Boring Weevil –
Euophryum sp

In Ireland, *Pentarthrum huttoni* Wollaston is the longest established species but it was first recorded only in 1926. In Dublin, large numbers have been found infesting floorboards in a house set out in flats. In 1985, adults were discovered in a Co Mayo hospital, which contained dry rot.

Euophryum confine Broun was recorded from Britain in 1937 and has since become widespread there, being extremely common in London. It was taken in this country in 1952 from a house at Rathmines in Dublin. Subsequent records include an adult emerging from the surface of a polished oak table indoors near Belfast, specimens collected in a dry rot-infested flat in Belfast and an adult embedded in a bar of soap in a 'digs' in Waterford. In one Dublin premises, large numbers were reported even crawling about on the beds. Very damp conditions were present and the weevils were apparently inhabiting the skirting boards.

Although known in Britain since 1934, the first Irish specimen of *Euophryum rufum* Broun was not obtained until 1976, when it was found by a health inspector in a bowl of sugar in a Dublin restaurant. Subsequently, an entire colony was found thriving in a rotting window frame in an old pub in Dublin's Temple Bar. Shortly afterwards, this population became extinct when the owner installed a new window.

Grain Weevils *Sitophilus* spp

The adults are small (2.5–5mm) and brown to dark brown or black. They are very noticeable when infesting pale-coloured foods such as rice and maize. The snout is long and the elbowed antennae end in distinct clubs. There are three species. The **grain weevil** (*Sitophilus granarius* (Linnaeus)) cannot fly because the wings are very reduced. The other two, which are very difficult to distinguish, are called the **maize weevil** or the **greater rice weevil** (*Sitophilus zeamais* Motschulsky) and the **lesser rice weevil** (*Sitophilus oryzae* (Linnaeus)) respectively—they are both winged, capable of flight and have two reddish spots on each wing-case.

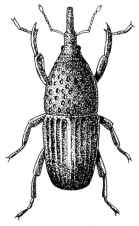

Grain Weevil –
Sitophilus granarius
(Linnaeus)

As its name suggests, the grain weevil is a very common pest in stored grain. A survey in Northern Ireland revealed that 12% of 274 local farm stores were infested, while in another year, 15% of stores were affected. Although unable to fly, the adults are tireless walkers. The egg is laid in a hole gnawed in a grain by the female. Over her life-time of several months, she can produce as many as three hundred eggs. The whitish legless larva or grub has a brown head. It feeds wholly inside the grain which is eventually hollowed out, leaving an empty husk. The species has caused losses in Irish intervention stores. It will also attack hard starch-containing products including dry biscuits and pasta. In houses, infestations usually arise from a packet of bird seed.

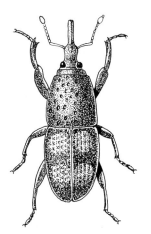

Lesser Rice Weevil –
Sitophilus oryzae
(Linnaeus)

The maize and rice weevils appear to be rarer in this country. *Sitophilus oryzae* has eaten maize and wheat in granaries and its continuous activity can cause grain to heat. Small numbers have been introduced into warehouses on rice or bran but the species is unable to survive in unheated buildings in Ireland. In a Dublin house in 1988, a dead specimen of *Sitophilus zeamais* was discovered in a bag of rice, an experience which is not unusual in Britain.

Holly Weevil   *Mesites tardii* (Curtis)

This large weevil (6–12mm) was first described as a new species when it was found in the old holly trees of Powerscourt Deerpark, Co Wicklow. It was named (in Latin) after its discoverer—the Irishman James Tardy. It is a wood-boring beetle that is sometimes brought into houses in firewood in which the immature stages are living prior to hatching. While the wood is being stored before burning, the beetles may emerge in large numbers. If this happens indoors, it can cause great worry, but the species is completely harmless and will not damage anything in a house.

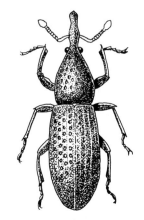

Holly Weevil –
Mesites tardii
(Curtis)

Mango Stone Weevil   *Sternochetus mangiferae* (Fabricius)

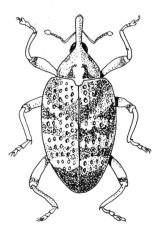

The large (6–9mm) adult is dark brown with paler patches. The white legless larva has a brown head. A tropical species, it attacks the mango fruit and is occasionally imported into Ireland. It lives inside the seed within the stone. The weevil usually emerges after the fruit is harvested and may turn up in importers' warehouses, shops or houses. In 1978 live ones were found in a mango in Co Galway. Subsequently, another turned up alive in a mango purchased in Sutton, Co Dublin, when the customer idly cracked open the stone after eating the fruit at home. The slow-moving adult is completely harmless and an inn-keeper in Co Wicklow recently kept one as a pet in a jam jar, feeding it regularly with fresh fruit.

Mango Stone Weevil –
Sternochetus mangiferae
(Fabricius)

Bark Beetles   Family: Scolytidae

The majority of species live in the twigs, branches and trunks of trees and some are serious pests, transmitting plant diseases.

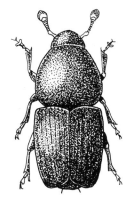

Large Elm Bark Beetle –
Scolytus scolytus
(Fabricius)

Large Elm Bark Beetle *Scolytus scolytus* **(Fabricius)**

The adults (3–6mm) occur from April to August. The head and thorax are black while the wing-cases are reddish. The body shape is characteristic.

The larvae live between the bark and sapwood of elm trees. Although first found as recently as 1943 on the Kenmare Estate, Killarney, Co Kerry, the species is now widely distributed. Specimens were probably brought into this country in infested wood. These beetles carry the fungus causing Dutch elm disease, which has destroyed elms throughout Ireland. Occasionally, live adults are found in houses after emerging from elm logs brought inside for use as firewood. However, apart from carrying the Dutch elm fungus, they are harmless and will not cause any damage indoors.

Ash Bark Beetle *Lepersinus varius* **(Fabricius)**

The ash bark beetle is a small (2.5–3.5mm) blackish species. This insect can be abundant in ash logs cut the previous winter for firewood.

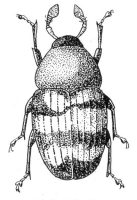

Ash Bark Beetle –
Lepersinus varius
(Fabricius)

False Powder-Post Beetles   Family: Bostrychidae

Bamboo Borer or 'Ghoon' Beetle *Dinoderus* spp

The adults are small (2.5–3mm) and reddish brown to blackish brown in colour. The head is hooded by the prothorax, which often has spines on it. Spines may also be present on the ends of the wing-cases.

These beetles frequent the warmer and mostly tropical regions of the world. In the wild, the white or pale yellow larvae feed mainly inside bamboo, although there are records from other timbers. When the wood is harvested, it is often used for furniture or other household objects, which are then exported to foreign countries including Ireland. The appearance of small holes along with 'sawdust', caused by the emerging beetles, is usually the first indication of an infestation.

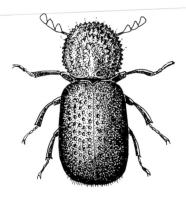

Bamboo Borer –
Dinoderus sp

In severe infestations, the wood may be almost completely hollowed out. In Ireland, bamboo furniture has had rather a bad reputation. This may be due to problems with these insects in the past, before suitable chemical treatments for the wood became available.

Four species have been reported from this country. *Dinoderus brevis* Horn occurred in imported rattan furniture in 1989. *Dinoderus minutus* (Fabricius) occurred with the previous species but it also extensively damaged Taiwanese chop-sticks purchased in a Dublin store. The two other species were taken in dunnage (mats and brushwood used to prevent moisture and chafing in a cargo) at Dublin docks and in bamboo poles.

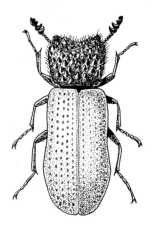

Capuchin Borer *Bostrychus capucinus* **(Linnaeus)**

The adult is a large (6–15mm) distinctive-looking insect with its black thorax and red wing-cases. The larvae live in oak sapwood and the wood of fruit trees. The beetles have been found in Irish premises after emerging from imported wooden objects.

Capuchin Borer –
Bostrychus capucinus
(Linnaeus)

Lesser Grain Borer   *Rhizopertha dominica* (Fabricius)

The small adults (2.5–3mm) have a blackish thorax and brownish wing-cases. It is a cosmopolitan pest of starch-rich grains, tubers, seeds and their ground or semi-manufactured products. The diet includes wheat, barley, rice, maize, millet, sorghum, dried potatoes and biscuits.

In Ireland, it can only survive in heated buildings. Interestingly, an adult was taken on a coat sleeve on a tram in Dublin in 1929. Presumably, the person had come from an infested building. It has been recorded in a corn-store in Limerick.

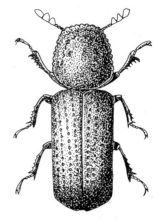

Lesser Grain Borer –
Rhizopertha dominica
(Fabricus)

Darkling Beetles   Family: Tenebrionidae

Lesser Mealworm Beetle   *Alphitobius diaperinus* (Panzer)

The adults are black and about 6mm long. The species occurs in stored flour and other cereal products but is not regarded as a primary pest there, normally infesting only mouldy or otherwise

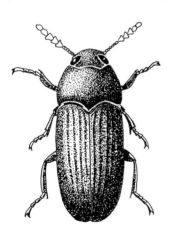

damaged goods. It has been brought into Ireland in animal feeding stuffs and such importations may be responsible for many of the infestations here. One such shipment of pollard and wheat pellets originated in West Africa.

Although they usually require heated premises to survive throughout the year, there are records of populations living through winter conditions in unheated buildings in this part of the world. In one Irish mill, a population lasted for three years in a damp, heated basement and often attained considerable numbers. In Northern Ireland, the species inhabited provender mills from where it was carried to farms.

Lesser Mealworm Beetle –
Alphitobius diaperinus
(Panzer)

It can be a serious pest in piggeries and poultry houses, destroying polystyrene or Styrofoam sheets used for insulation.

Holes are made by the mature white larvae seeking pupation sites and in France, the resultant lost of heat has affected the profitability of such units. There are Irish records also of damage of this type from Counties Cork and Monaghan.

Specimens are often found in large numbers in the deep litter of poultry houses and the species has been implicated as a possible carrier of poultry disease. The lesser mealworm beetle may eat dead or moribund chickens.

Flour Beetles *Tribolium* spp

There are several species of flour beetle and it requires expert knowledge to identify them. However, the two common Irish species may be distinguished by the shape of the antennae in the adults. In the **confused flour beetle** (*Tribolium confusum* du Val), the antennae gradually widen to the tip, while in the **rust-red flour beetle** (*Tribolium castaneum* (Herbst)), they end in a distinct three-segmented club. The adults are small (3–4mm), reddish brown and rather flat.

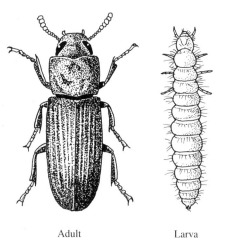

Adult   Larva

Confused Flour Beetle –
Tribolium confusum
Du Val

Both types of flour beetle can live for six hundred days, and four to five hundred eggs may be laid. The yellowish white larvae reach 6mm and have two upturned, dark, pointed structures at the end of the body.

(Head of)
Rust-Red Flour Beetle –
Tribolium castaneum
(Herbst)

As the common names suggest, both adults and larvae live in flour and cereal products, but they do not appear to attack sound grain. Infested flour has a greyish colour, however, and has a tendency to go mouldy. Other foodstuffs are attacked, including beans, dried fruit, spices and chocolate.

In Britain, the rust-red flour beetle is the most commonly intercepted pest insect on many kinds of imported food, especially oilseed, oilcake and rice bran. A female can find her way into even tightly closed packets of food, and householders may find these insects in purchased products due to poor hygiene practices in mills and bakeries.

In unheated buildings in Ireland this beetle cannot survive the winter. It persists in this country, not by becoming established but by repeated contamination from infested imported commodities. Irish records of the rust-red flour beetle include the rice-store of a hospital and in imported pollard pellets from Ghana. In one instance, both adults and larvae were discovered in an Irish-manufactured cereal which was exported to Cyprus. The product was returned following a complaint, but it may have become contaminated during transportation or storage. In 1986, larvae of the confused flour beetle turned up in a baby's feeding bottle in Dublin. The bottle contained a solution of baby food.

Yellow Mealworm Beetle *Tenebrio molitor* (Linnaeus)

These large (12–17.5mm) beetles range in colour from reddish brown to black. Both larvae and adults feed on cereals and their products. Scraps of meat and dead insects are also attacked. An adult was even found on one occasion in a sample of Irish-grown tobacco.

Known as mealworms, the larvae are a popular food for pets such as birds and reptiles. Growing to 28mm, they may survive for nine months without any food or moisture. When mature, they wander about looking for a suitable pupation site and may then end up accidentally in bags or packages of other products.

The species is slow-growing, thriving in dark and damp places. Infestations are generally indicative of poor hygiene, though they may arise from birds' nests. Customers found larvae baked in bread purchased in a shop in Dublin in 1985.

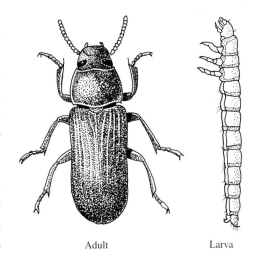

Adult   Larva

Yellow Mealworm Beetle –
Tenebrio molitor
(Linnaeus)

65

Dark Mealworm Beetle *Tenebrio obscurus* **Fabricius**

The dark mealworm beetle is uncommon in Ireland, being associated mainly with flour-mills, grain stores and stables, though it can be found in other premises. There is an 1860 record from dry flour in Co Down. It is also known from Dublin and Wicklow. It can be easily distinguished from the yellow mealworm beetle in the larval stage: those of *T. molitor* are shining yellow while those of *T. obscurus* are tinged with brown.

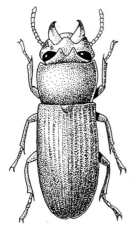

Broad-Horned Flour Beetle –
Gnatocerus cornutus
(Fabricius)

Broad-Horned Flour Beetle *Gnatocerus cornutus* **(Fabricius)**

The males of these small (3.5–5mm) red beetles are very distinctive, possessing large teeth (mandibles) which curve upwards. The white larvae have no tail-horns.

A cosmopolitan species, it is mainly a pest of flour and meal but can live on grains and bone meal. It is fairly common in Britain, occurring in flour mills, and there are also records from Irish mills. It has also infested bakeries here, but the species does not survive in these islands in unheated buildings. Like the lesser mealworm beetle, this species has been known to damage polystyrene insulation in Irish piggeries by tunnelling.

Small-Eyed Flour Beetle *Palorus ratzeburgi* **(Wissmann)**
and

Depressed Flour Beetle *Palorus subdepressus* **(Wollaston)**

The adults are small (2.5–3mm) and reddish. These beetles and their larvae infest grain, flour and bran often in large numbers but can also occur in the wild under the bark of old deciduous trees.

There is a recent record of an infestation of *P. ratzeburgi* in a kitchen in Cork city and both species have been reported from granaries and flour mills in this country.

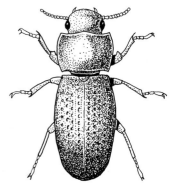

Small-Eyed Flour Beetle –
Palorus ratzeburgi
(Wissmann)

Cellar Beetle *Blaps mucronata* Latreille

Also known as the churchyard beetle, the adult is large (18–25mm), flightless and almost shining black in colour. The beetle is nocturnal, living in or near buildings, storehouses, sheds and cellars, where it will feed on almost any food. Damp, dark places are preferred. When alarmed, it can emit a foul smell.

The larva also has a varied diet but will not eat meat. It can occur in spilt or damaged food debris but is not specifically a food pest. Resembling a mealworm, the body ends in a single upturned dark spine rather than in two.

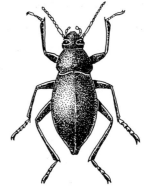

Cellar Beetle –
Blaps mucronata
Latreille

Although recorded from only six Irish counties at the turn of the century, the cellar beetle was then considered to be common in cellars and outhouses. It now appears to be rare, although there are recent records from houses and a warehouse in Dublin. The decline in this beetle may be due to the damp-proofing of older buildings, coupled with the lack of cellars and the improvements in the construction of modern housing.

Interestingly, another species (*Blaps lethifera* Marsham) was discovered during the excavations of Viking Dublin at Wood Quay in 1978. The remains of two beetles (a male and a female) were found associated with tenth- and eleventh-century structures. One specimen showed damage possibly caused by an angry Viking who had found it indoors. They were probably imported in a cargo.

In Britain, *Blaps lethifera* is a rare insect, invariably linked with human habitation. In a case we read of, the species was numerous in chaff and debris under a grain bin and old sacks in the corner of a stable in Suffolk, in 1981.

Grain Beetles   Family: Silvanidae

This family includes two important species, the **merchant grain beetle**, *Oryzaephilus mercator* (Fauvel), and the **saw-toothed grain beetle**, *Oryzaephilus surinamensis* (Linnaeus). Adults of these two small (2.5–3.5mm) species are black or dark brown. Characteristically, they have a series of serrations or tooth-like protuberances on each side of the thorax.

The female produces an average of 170 eggs, which are laid in crevices in or near the food material. The larvae are yellowish with brown flecks and a brown head, reaching 3mm in length; their excrement can contaminate the food source.

Common in both temperate and warm areas of the world, these pests have been known to survive Irish winters even in unheated buildings.

They are serious pests of stored products of vegetable origin including cereals (rice, wheat, barley, maize) or their products (bread, pasta). Infestations of dried fruit (such as currants, raisins, sultanas) are common. On one occasion in Ireland, over forty tons of Greek dried currants had to be destroyed because of infestation. Drugs are also attacked.

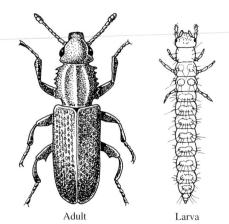

Adult   Larva

Saw-Toothed Grain Beetle –
Oryzaephilus surinamensis
(Linnaeus)

Their small size enables them to hide in crevices inaccessible to sprays and fumigants. If left unchecked, these species can spread through a grocery store and cause serious damage. In houses, specimens can be brought indoors as a contaminant of purchased goods. They are serious pests also of farm-stored grain which may become mouldy or sprout.

In 1981 in Cork, *O. surinamensis* caused major problems in intervention stores. In the same county, both species infested rice and other food in hospital kitchens and storage areas.

Rove Beetles   Family: Staphylinidae

There are some thousand species of rove beetle in Britain and Ireland, but they are seldom pests. All have short wing-cases, unlike the majority of beetles, exposing most of the abdomen.

Fly-in-the-Eye Beetle   *Anotylus tetracarinatus*   **(Block)**

The small (1.7–2.2mm) black adult is very common in Ireland and can occur in very large numbers. The popular name is derived from its habit of accidentally flying into the eyes of humans, particularly cyclists. This species may be the most abundant of all European beetles, living in dung and soil, under rotting vegetable matter, in excrement and in birds' nests. When the beetles are swarming on sunny days, they may fly indoors. An office infestation of adults in Dublin, for example, was traced to the neglected garbage of a nearby restaurant.

Devil's Coach-Horse   *Ocypus olens* (Müller)

The fearsome-looking adults are large (22–32mm) and pitch black. One could easily imagine a team of them pulling a miniature coach containing a devil or goblin—hence the popular name.

Although a common Irish insect, this beetle is not often noticed, since it is nocturnal. During the day, it hides under stones or other suitable objects. When it ventures out at night, it is an aggressive predator with a preference for attacking earthworms, but it will also eat slugs and other small creatures.

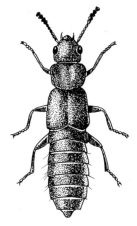

Fly-in-the-Eye Beetle –
Anotylus tetracarinatus
(Block)

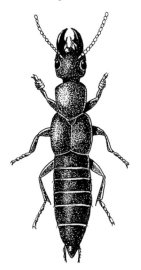

Devil's Coach-Horse –
Ocypus olens
(Müller)

Sometimes while hunting, it may accidentally wander indoors. Upon discovering a specimen, many householders' first reaction is to poke it and the frightened beetle will respond by bending its abdomen upwards like a scorpion, making it both fierce-looking and ready to spray some noxious chemical. However, it is all bluff and the insect is harmless. Another name (cock-the-tail) is derived from this behaviour (in the north of Ireland, it is called the coffin cutter from the undeserved idea that it burrows into graves and eats its way through the coffins).

In 1994, there was a population explosion of these insects and many were submitted for identification from all over the country, but numbers have now once again returned to normal.

Seed Beetles   Family: Bruchidae

Pea and Bean Beetles   *Bruchus* spp

The small (4–5mm) globular adults have distinctively shortened wing-cases which expose the end of the body.

They are also called bruchids or pulse beetles. There are
several different species which attack leguminous seeds or
dried stored seeds. Their diet includes peas, beans and other
lentils. The larvae bore into seeds and eat them from inside.
When mature, they pupate inside and the beetles may not
emerge for some time. As a result, specimens can emerge from
purchased products, producing a characteristic round hole in
the seed. Records have become commoner as consumers
switch to a healthier diet by eating more of these vegetables,
particularly imported ones. Individuals can also be brought
indoors in plant seeds (such as those of lupins). The earliest
Irish record is from imported French beans in 1899.

Pea and Bean Beetle –
Bruchus sp

Leaf Beetles   Family: Chrysomelidae

Colorado Beetle   *Leptinotarsa decemlineata* (Say)

The large (8–12mm), distinctive-looking adults have alternating yellow and black stripes on the
wing-cases. The equally distinctive larvae are bright pink, with two rows of black spots on each
side of the body.

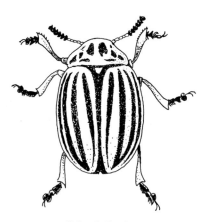

Colorado Beetle –
Leptinotarsa decemlineata
(Say)

The Colorado beetle is a notorious pest of potatoes,
and will also attack tomatoes, peppers and other
related plants. The adults hibernate in the soil for the
duration of the winter and emerge in early summer. On
warm days they fly off in search of potato and related
host plants. Each female lays an average of five to
eight hundred eggs, which hatch within a few days.
Infested plants can be reduced to skeletons of bare
stems, fouled by black excrement. On the continent,
severe infestations cause substantial or complete loss
of crops.

Originating in the western USA, the Colorado beetle
was accidentally introduced into France in 1922 and is

now widely distributed in Europe, though it has not yet reached Britain or Ireland. However, specimens have sometimes been found in imported goods in Ireland, including in Spanish chipboard, Italian parsley and celery and French grain. In one instance, live adults were seen walking along the checkout counter of a supermarket.

Although not an indoor pest, and in any case not established in Ireland, this species is included here because of its potential importance to Irish agriculture, were it to become established here. If this were to happen, this pest would cause severe economic losses for Irish farmers. If you do discover any specimens, please notify the Department of Agriculture immediately.

Flea Beetles *Phyllotreta* spp

These small (1.5–3mm) beetles have stout hind legs modified for jumping—hence the popular name. Some have a yellow band on the wing-case, while others are completely bronze, bluish, greenish or black. Many species are pests of crops or garden plants and are common Irish insects.

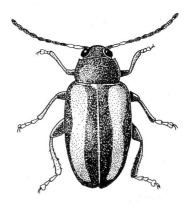

Flea Beetle –
Phyllotreta sp

As well as eating leaves, they can transmit viral diseases. The larvae feed on roots, or mine leaves. The beetles hibernate through the winter in plant debris under hedges, in grass tussocks, under loose bark on trees and in similar situations. They emerge in early spring and move on to young plants to feed. The next generation occurs in August–October.

The adults may occur in large numbers in crops and since they can fly for a kilometre or more, they sometimes accidentally enter nearby houses. Because of their jumping behaviour, they have been mistaken by Irish householders and health inspectors for fleas, but are harmless to humans.

Scarab Beetles   Family: Scarabaeidae

Cockchafer   *Melolontha* spp

There are two very common and similar looking species in Ireland—*Melolontha melolontha* (Linnaeus) and *M. hippocastani* Fabricius. The distinctive adults are large (20–30mm) and mainly brown. They are also popularly known as maybugs.

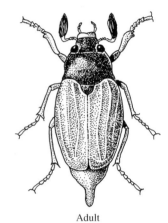

Adult

Cockchafer –
Melolontha melolontha
(Linnaeus)

Cockchafers or maybugs feed mostly on the leaves, flowers and fruit of deciduous plants, normally causing little damage in this country. However, a plague of cockchafers was recorded in the west of Ireland during the summer of 1688 and caused great damage there: 'The whole country... was left as bare and naked as it had been in the depth of winter, making a most unseemly and indeed frightful appearance.' Eventually, a change in the weather killed them off.

The larvae or 'rookworms' are very destructive pests, attacking roots. Large numbers can build up in neglected permanent grassland. They can cause serious problems in crops, lawns and golf courses.

Larva

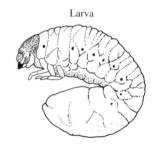

At dusk in late spring and early summer, adults are sometimes seen in huge swarms around the tops of trees and shrubs. They make a very distinctive humming sound in flight. On warm evenings, they are often attracted indoors by lights and can cause consternation among the inhabitants but they are completely harmless.

The adults are among the most frequent insects submitted for identification by the Irish public. In one case here, a housewife found cockchafers in her house and incorrectly assumed that they were emerging from the woodwork. She contacted a disreputable pest firm which sprayed her house and charged her several hundred pounds for this totally unnecessary treatment—the beetles had originated in woodland at the back of her house, flying indoors through open windows. The problem was easily solved by closing the windows.

Dung Beetles   Family: Geotrupidae

Dung beetles belonging to various families are often attracted to lights indoors. They are completely harmless. One common species is described here.

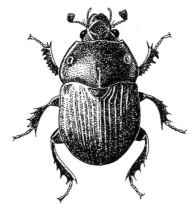

Dor Beetle   *Geotrupes stercorarius* (Linnaeus)

The adult is a large (16–26mm), distinctive-looking, black insect. It is common in Ireland from April to October and has a preference for horse dung. Other popular names are 'dumble dor', 'clock' and 'lousy watchman', this last name referring to the mites which infest the underside of the beetle.

Dor Beetle –
Geotrupes stercorarius
(Linnaeus)

Predacious Diving Beetles   Family: Dytiscidae

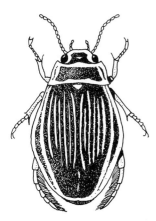

Predacious Diving Beetle –
Dytiscidae

Like dung beetles, harmless water beetles belonging to various families are often attracted by lights. The dytiscids are a typical example. Varying in size (1.5mm–35mm), the adults have a distinctive shape. Both the beetles and the larvae eat insects and other small animals in water-bodies.

One specimen submitted as a pest by a housewife in Co Wexford proved to be new to Ireland. It probably entered the house by mistake during migration. During hot weather, large numbers of water beetles can land on motor cars and die. It seems that they mistake the reflection from certain paints for water.

Ground Beetles   Family: Carabidae

This is a large family of Irish insects, which vary greatly in size (*c.* 2–35mm). The adults have a characteristic shape and are often black. Most are nocturnal, hiding under stones and similar objects during the day-time.

Both adults and larvae eat insects, slugs, worms and other small animals. A few species attack strawberries. Being adept at squeezing through narrow spaces, they may accidentally enter houses at night and can be found wandering about on the floor. They are harmless to humans.

Ground Beetle –
Carabidae

However, for unknown reasons, outdoor populations may explode and the numbers coming indoors can reach plague proportions. In Britain, in an incident we read about, five to six hundred beetles entered a particular house each night. A similar problem was experienced by householders in the Navan Road area of Dublin city during the 1960s. For a period of several weeks, hundreds of beetles crawled into houses over a wide area, greatly distressing the inhabitants. As a defence, these beetles give off a sharp sourish smell when alarmed. In the first days of the infestation, many people stamped on the beetles occurring in their houses, producing a most unpleasant and persistent smell. In the end, they found that the best solution was to sweep out any beetles that were found during daylight. As suddenly as it had exploded, the beetle population returned to normal and the problem has not recurred.

Chequered Beetles   Family: Cleridae

Red-Legged Copra Beetle   *Necrobia rufipes* **(De Geer)**

The adults range from 4 to 8mm and are greenish blue with reddish legs. The larvae reach a length of 10mm. The life-cycle can be completed within a month.

Although also a carrion-eater, this insect was spread around the world by the trade in copra (dried coconut). In Britain, the species is a pest in factories and warehouses, attacking concentrated fodder, copra, palm kernels and other oilseeds, fish and bone meal, milk and egg powder. Pharmaceutical products may be also damaged.

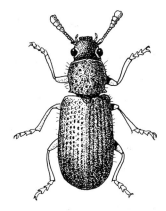

The female may lay as many as three hundred eggs but the average is two hundred. The larvae bore into the food, but they can survive for sixty-two days without food. There are Irish records from Counties Antrim, Down and Dublin.

A similar species, the **red-breasted copra beetle** (*Necrobia ruficollis* (Fabricius)) has also been found here.

Red-Legged Copra Beetle – *Necrobia rufipes* (De Geer)

Flat Grain Beetles   Family: Cucujidae

Rust-Red Grain Beetle   *Cryptolestes ferrugineus*   (Stephens)

These small (1.25–2.5mm) red beetles attack grain, flour, flour products and dried fruit. The larvae reach 4mm in length and the life-cycle can be completed in under two months.

They can spread through and spoil bulk foodstuffs. Indeed in Britain, this species is one of the most important pests of farm-stored grain. Over four thousand individuals have been reported from a kilogram of grain.

This beetle can also occur in houses and there have been infestations in Irish intervention stores and also in mills, where it is one of the commonest insects inside machinery. A survey was undertaken in Northern Ireland in 1942–6, which showed that large numbers developed in dock silos during the summertime and cross-infestation took place on a number of occasions, sometimes by insects walking from one bin to another, and sometimes by a residual infestation remaining in a bin after the infested grain was removed. The species has also been imported in dried fruit from Australia.

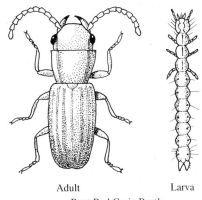

Adult   Larva

Rust-Red Grain Beetle –
Cryptolestes ferrugineus
(Stephens)

Another species, *C. pusillus* (Schoenherr), has also been found in Ireland.

75

Powder-Post Beetles   Family: Lyctidae

Brown Powder-Post Beetle   *Lyctus brunneus* (Stephens)

The adults are brown and very slender and range in size from 2.2 to 7mm. The creamy white larvae, which reach 5mm, burrow in the sapwood of susceptible hardwoods until nothing is left but a fine powder—hence the popular name. Only a thin veneer may remain on the outside. Coniferous wood is not attacked.

This species is becoming a serious pest because of changes in the way timber is seasoned. Instead of being left to cure for years, it is often dried by heat soon after the tree has been felled, leaving cells still containing starch. It is now an important pest in Britain, attacking parquet floors and oak panelling in houses.

The beetles are attracted to light and during an infestation, they will be often seen crawling on windows. It was first reported here in 1949 from imported Australian boxes containing tinned sweets. Subsequent Irish records include beetles emerging in a house from an Italian mirror purchased two years previously and an infestation in Italian picture frames imported from New Zealand. Fortunately, this pest still appears to be unestablished in this country.

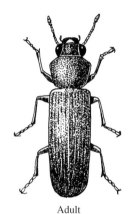

Adult

Brown Powder-Post Beetle –
Lyctus brunneus
(Stephens)

Larva

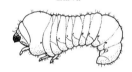

Trogossitid Beetles   Family: Trogossitidae

Cadelle Beetle   *Tenebroides mauritanicus* (Linnaeus)

The brownish to black adult is one of the larger beetles (5–11mm) to be found in flour mills, where it feeds on flour and also on other insects. The white larva has a black head, two black patches on the thorax and two prominent horns on the end of the body. The fully grown larvae may bore into surrounding woodwork.

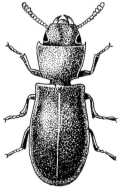

Adult

Cadelle Beetle –
Tenebroides mauritanicus
(Linnaeus)

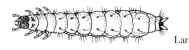

Larva

This species originated in Africa but has been spread around the world. It has been known to bite holes in cloth used as a mesh for bolting (sieving) flour. In Ireland, it has been reported in appreciable numbers from flour and other mills. Occasionally, it is found in warehouses. There is a recent record from pollard pellets imported into Louth from Ghana.

Longhorn Beetles   Family: Cerambycidae

Most species in this family have long feelers (antennae). A wide variety of species have been imported into Ireland in wood, and adults are occasionally found indoors. A species which could cause problems if it becomes established here is described below.

House Longhorn Beetle   *Hylotrupes bajulus* (Linnaeus)

The adults are very variable in size (7–25mm) and are greyish brown to black with greyish hairs. They are distinctive in appearance.

The species attacks dry coniferous timbers, especially in the roof voids and attics of houses. As a result, it is an important pest of structural timbers in Europe. It also occurs in packing-cases and infestations may arise from such sources. The female can lay four hundred eggs and the larvae live inside the wood for several years, feeding mainly on sapwood. They are a shiny ivory white in colour and can reach up to 24mm in length. The exit holes may be the first evidence of an attack, although the rasping sounds of the larvae gnawing through the timbers can alert householders to their presence in lofts.

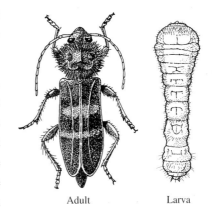

Adult   Larva

House Longhorn Beetle –
Hylotrupes bajulus
(Linnaeus)

The species now appears to be established in north-west Surrey in England and it has turned up in Ireland in introduced timber.

Chapter 5: Flies—Order: Diptera

God in His wisdom

Made the fly

And then forgot

To tell us why.

Ogden Nash[5]

Hoverflies   Family: Syrphidae

Drone Fly   *Eristalis tenax* **(Linnaeus)**

The drone fly resembles the honeybee but has only a single pair of wings. It is a large insect (15mm) and belongs to the hover-flies, a group famous for their flying skills, including the ability to hover in mid-air. The adults are valuable pollinators of flowers and are completely harmless.

However, the drone fly can cause problems. Known as rat-tailed maggots, the immature stages inhabit organically polluted drains and ditches where foul water and other liquids often accumulate after draining from silage pits, manure heaps, creameries, abattoirs and similar situations. The young thrive in such conditions, sometimes resulting in large numbers of adults

Adult

Drone Fly –
Eristalis tenax
(Linnaeus)

Rat-Tailed Maggot – Larva

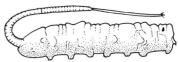

5 Zoo, 1987,
Stewart, Tabori
& Chang, New
York.

entering buildings where they are mistaken for an invasion of bees. The Natural History Museum was contacted about such an incident in Clonbrock House, Co Galway in 1976. In addition, the maggots can block toilets by clogging the pipes. They are easily recognised. Whitish in colour and reaching 32mm in length, they have a long telescopic tail used for reaching the surface to obtain oxygen from the air. When mature, the maggots migrate, looking for a drier place in which to pupate. During their search, they can travel as far as 30 metres and become a nuisance in nearby buildings by climbing interior walls. In creameries, they may enter empty milk bottles and have been known to contaminate milk in Ireland.

Blowflies   Family: Calliphoridae

Bluebottle *Calliphora* spp

Dull metallic blue in colour, the adults can be 11mm long with a wing span of 25mm. Bluebottles are very familiar insects in Ireland, frequently entering houses, where they are detested by the housekeeper and cook. The heavy buzzing of the females as they clumsily career round a room portends the 'blowing' of food. With an uncanny instinct to locate meat in spite of extraordinary obstacles, bluebottles are a common cause of food-poisoning in this country.

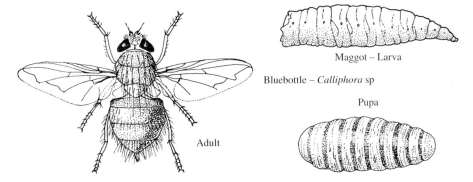

Maggot – Larva

Bluebottle – *Calliphora* sp

Pupa

Adult

Very characteristic of the warmer months, bluebottles are often associated with garbage. They prefer to breed in decaying matter of animal origin, including corpses, but if necessary animal faeces and rotting vegetable material will be used. A female is capable of laying two hundred eggs, but some species instead produce live young. There are three white worm-like larval or maggot stages, known as 'gentles' by fishermen. When they reach maturity—which under favourable circumstances can be achieved in a week—the maggots (c. 18mm) migrate, usually at night, and can travel 25–30m.

Pupation occurs in the soil, in cracks or under objects. The pupae are dull red–brown and short–cylindrical in shape. Intestinal myiasis as a result of eating food containing maggots is occasionally reported from humans. However, such cases are rare, suggesting that the young stages do not survive well in our intestines. Live maggots have been found in babies' nappies, however.

Occasionally, large infestations of adults have been reported in Ireland after small rodents had been poisoned indoors. The body of a mouse, for example, may provide sufficient nutriment to breed some two to five hundred individuals. A householder may be plagued for weeks by adults emerging from under the floorboards, attracted by light.

In houses, the numbers of these pests can be reduced through using refrigerators and secure cupboards for the storage of meat or other foods and by careful attention to dustbin hygiene.

Greenbottle   *Lucilia* spp

The adults are very variable in size (5–10mm long), depending on the nutriment available to the young. According to age, the colour ranges from a deep bluish green with violet reflections to an emerald-green with darker green reflections.

Greenbottles lay their eggs in excrement or decaying animal matter and are often attracted to fish. Unlike the bluebottles, greenbottles are seldom attracted indoors.

Sheep Maggot Fly   *Lucilia sericata* (Meigen)

The sheep maggot fly is a common species and, as its name implies, this insect is normally associated with sheep and attacks open wounds or wet or faeces-soiled fleece, particularly around the tail area. The maggots live on the living flesh and, if the infestation is left untreated, the sheep can die.

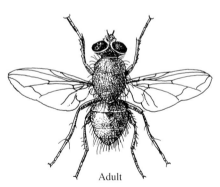

Adult

Sheep Maggot Fly –
Lucilia sericata
(Meigen)

The species is also attracted to ill humans who have soiled themselves while in a coma or similar situation and are unable to look after themselves. Laid near the anus, eggs hatch in about eight hours at normal human temperatures. The maggots then enter the rectum where they

Larva

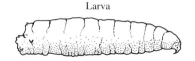

complete their development within three days. Any maggots noted leaving the anus have actually finished feeding and are looking for a pupation site.

On the credit side, these insects restrict themselves to dead tissue in humans and may stimulate the healing process by their excretions. This has led to their surgical use in hospitals.

Cluster Flies   Families: Calliphoridae and Muscidae

Indoors, several species of flies can cause problems by hibernating together in large numbers. Adults will often travel several miles to cluster in a particular building. It is not known why this happens. In a district, the same house will be selected year after year. An infestation is usually not noticed until springtime, when the adults wake up and congregate on windows, trying to escape.

Cluster Fly   *Pollenia rudis* (Fabricius)

The commonest species in Ireland, the adult is a large (10mm) greyish black fly. The young live inside earthworms. In the autumn, adults may be observed sunning themselves on walls. As the weather turns cold, they seek shelter under eaves, in attics or upstairs rooms. When conditions become milder in spring, the sudden appearance of adults in large numbers flying about indoors can cause consternation. However, the damage caused by these insects is normally negligible although some staining

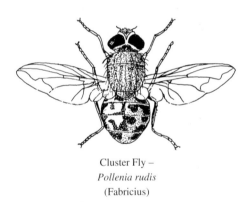

Cluster Fly –
Pollenia rudis
(Fabricius)

to paintwork and wallpaper may occur. Cluster flies can be eliminated by opening windows to provide an escape route and by vacuuming up any dead ones.

Cluster Fly   *Dasyphora cyanella* (Meigen)

Another widespread species, these flies resemble greenbottles, but differ in having two dark longitudinal marks along the thorax. The immature stages live in cow-dung.

House Flies   Family: Muscidae

House Fly   *Musca domestica* **Linnaeus**

The common house fly is usually 6–7mm long with a 13–15mm wing span. The grey thorax has four longitudinal stripes, while the sides of the basal half of the abdomen are yellowish buff with a central dark band.

The adults breed in a diverse range of substances, provided they are moist, fermenting or rotting. Examples include excrement, decaying vegetable matter and garbage. A single female can lay a hundred to a hundred and fifty eggs at a time, repeating this process at intervals.

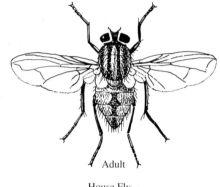

Adult

House Fly –
Musca domestica
Linnaeus

Larva

The young larvae or maggots dislike light and burrow into their food. The three larval stages all resemble whitish cones, with the mouth at the pointed end. They breathe through two openings

in the blunt hind part. When mature, the maggots may wander about looking for a suitable pupation site. The pupa forms within the hardened brown larval skin. The life-cycle may be completed within three weeks.

The adults frequently cause disease in Ireland, especially because of poor hygiene. They feed by first vomiting over their food. Enzymes then break it down and the resultant liquid or broth is sucked up. At the same time, excrement is voided. Although the vomit may transmit disease, excrement is the main source of contamination, as it contains bacteria such as *Salmonella*.

We have often noted these insects crawling about on bread, cakes and other foods in restaurants and shops in Ireland. Even the Victorians were aware of the necessity of covering food, and with the modern availability of suitable kitchen and display equipment, lapses in hygiene like this are inexcusable.

Lesser House Fly   *Fannia canicularis*
(Linnaeus)

The lesser house fly also occurs indoors. It is smaller than the house fly and its flight is very characteristic. Adults spend most of their time erratically flying around lamps and other ceiling fittings. The species breeds in moist decaying organic matter especially chicken dung. Its behaviour rarely results in contact with human food and, unlike the common house fly, it does not transmit diseases.

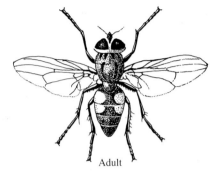

Adult

Lesser House Fly –
Fannia canicularis
(Linnaeus)

Larva

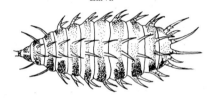

Stable Fly   *Stomoxys calcitrans* (Linnaeus)

The stable fly is also called the biting housefly because it is related to and resembles the common housefly. The body is greyish with indistinct blackish banding. The wings are clear without any distinct markings. The legs are dark brown to black. The eyes are large and dull and reddish in colour. The adult is easily distinguished from the housefly by the presence of biting mouth-parts recognisable as a short needle-like proboscis projecting from the front of the head. The adult is 6–7mm in length with a wing span of 15–17mm.

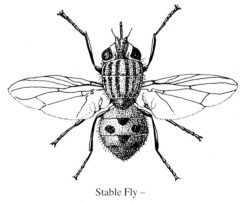

Stable Fly –
Stomoxys calcitrans
(Linnaeus)

The egg is oval and about 1.1mm long. As many as one hundred and fifty to four hundred and fifty can be laid in manure, rotting vegetation and decaying straw and bedding of farm animals, especially if soiled

83

by dung and/or urine. The hatching maggots, which resemble those of the housefly, feed on this material. A maggot can reach c. 11mm and, when fully mature, finds a drier place in which to pupate. At 16°C, the life-cycle can take about 58 days, but can be completed in 12 days at 30°C.

The adults, both males and females, take regular blood meals, attacking mainly cattle. However, they will also bite horses, pigs, dogs and humans. The blood is required for the maturation of the eggs. Feeding only during daytime, they can take in three times their body weight. People can be bitten both indoors and outdoors, and socks may be pierced. The bite is very painful.

Because of the larval habitat, stable flies are mainly a problem in rural areas, but there are records of people being attacked in suburban Dublin. The most likely area to find the species is in and around farmyards, stables, barns, outbuildings and farmhouses. The adults are often more persistent after rain.

Stable flies are capable of transmitting poliomyelitis and are suspected of being transmitters of trypanosomes to animals and humans. They are also implicated in the spread of anthrax, tularemia and other diseases.

Bird-Keds   Family: Hippoboscidae

Swift and Swallow Parasitic Fly *Crataerina pallida*
(Latreille)

The bird-ked is a flattened and ugly-looking fly. It is a common parasite of the swallow, swift and house-martin and infestations can occur in their nests under the eaves of buildings. In one Dublin flat, the flies came indoors through a ventilation shaft where birds had nested. They can bite humans.

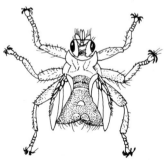

Swift and Swallow Parasitic Fly –
Crataerina pallida
(Latreille)

Piophilids   Family: Piophilidae

Cheese-Skipper *Piophila casei* **(Linnaeus)**

The adults are small dark blue or black shiny flies with a body length of 2.5–4.0mm and a wingspan of *c.* 8mm.

This fly gets its common name of cheese-skipper from the fact that the larvae or maggots are able to hop or skip into the air, travelling up to 25cm at a time. This skipping is accomplished by the maggot holding its rear end with its mouthparts and then suddenly letting go, causing it to skip, a rather useful mechanism to escape predators or angry cheese buffs.

Although associated with cheese, it can also affect other milk products as well as meat, offal, hides, furs and faeces. It is found on and in dry or cured high-protein foods and will travel deep into the food and excavate the interior. In the past it was not uncommon in shops selling cheese and smoked foods (especially ham, bacon and fish). Fortunately, it is now rather rare.

Cheese-Skipper –
Piophila casei
(Linnaeus)

The female fly can lay over two hundred eggs in a three- or four-day period. The eggs hatch in a few days into whitish maggots. On hatching, the maggots immediately bore into the food, making their presence difficult to detect unless there is a heavy infestation. In cured hams and bacon they are found deep inside, around the bone.

The mature maggot is about 6–8mm long and leaves the food to find a pupation site such as cracks or crevices in floors or walls, under boxes, etc. Under favourable conditions, the entire life-cycle can be completed in about two weeks.

The presence of these maggots in cheese was once regarded as a special mark of quality by gourmets but this is totally false and is indicative of bad hygiene and poor storage conditions. They are of considerable medical significance because the maggots, if consumed, can cause serious internal problems (myiasis, see page 153) by burrowing into the intestinal walls and are voided alive in the faeces.

Scuttle Flies   Family: Phoridae

These small black insects are easily recognised by their characteristic scuttling movements on windows and other surfaces.

Milkbottle Scuttle Fly   *Spiniphora bergenstammi* **(Mik)**

As its name suggests, this insect (adult about 3mm long) is sometimes found in milkbottles. The larvae live in snails, but they pupate elsewhere. A milkbottle left out at night is sometimes used as a site in which to pupate, perhaps after the bottle has fallen over on to its side. The larvae pupate after entering it, cementing themselves firmly to the inside. The glue-like secretion is so strong that it may resist the cleaning procedures in the washing plant and bottles with still-attached pupae can be filled with fresh milk. Their discovery usually results in consumers' complaints.

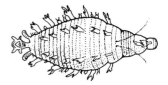

Pupa

Milkbottle Scuttle Fly –
Spiniphora bergenstammi
(Mik)

The pupa resembles a grain of wheat and there is an amusing story of a dairy representative eating one of these to demonstrate to an indignant housewife that it was harmless. The use of modern detergents seems to have considerably reduced the number of incidents in recent years. Adults occur from May to September, indicating that the problem with pupae should exist during the same period.

Fruit Flies and Vinegar Flies   Family: Drosophilidae

Of rather fat or bulbous appearance, these small (c. 2–5mm) insects are frequently seen by customers in Irish public houses where they are attracted to alcoholic drinks. Characteristically, they fly slowly around a glass before settling on the rim. The immature stages live in alcohol and other fermenting material such as rotting fruit. They may cause problems in restaurants and food factories.

Householders are frequently alarmed by the sudden emergence of numerous adults in kitchens and such infestations can usually be traced to some forgotten fruit in a cupboard. Similarly, they can hatch in large numbers from fruit discarded in garbage. They are sometimes noticed by homebrewers of wine when they become trapped in the air-locks of fermentation flasks. Certain species carry vinegar bacteria on their bodies and if these contaminate home-brewed wines and beers, they can result in home-brewed vinegar.

Kitchen Fly   *Drosophila repleta* Wollaston

The kitchen fly is a small grey–black insect which flies slowly and somewhat clumsily. It is a dangerous insect because, in addition to vegetable matter, it breeds in human excrement. The adults also feed on excrement and because of the species' strong attraction to this substance, it is frequently found in toilets and can occur in bed-pans.

Pupa

Kitchen Fly –
Drosophila repleta
Wollaston

Believed to be tropical in origin, it has only recently been reported from Ireland but may have been overlooked in the past. It has adapted to our indoor conditions and is spreading in this part of the world. In Britain, the kitchen fly is present in canteens, restaurants and public houses. By contrast, in Ireland, with one exception, the insect has only been reported from public houses, particularly those serving meals. The first record was from a Dublin city pub, where the adults occurred in a toilet. They were found resting on the ceiling and on the wall above the urinals. It is thought that the infestation originated in a nearby fast-food premises.

The exception is a Dublin house which had an indoor infestation. The adults probably entered the building on the clothes of one of the inhabitants and then found a source of food among stored fruit and vegetables in the kitchen.

The adults have a habit of alighting on white surfaces such as plates, sheets and tablecloths and can easily transmit disease organisms.

Milkbottle Fly   *Drosophila funebris* (Fabricius)

Like the milkbottle scuttle fly mentioned above, this species occurs in milkbottles. It breeds in those containing milk residues and the maggots may develop in the curds to the pupal stage before the bottles

Larva

Milkbottle Fly –
Drosophila funebris
(Fabricius)

Adult

are returned to the dairy. Sometimes, the ovoid pupae are not removed during the washing process and are subsequently overlooked. After the bottle is filled with fresh milk, they can float to the surface, resulting in complaints.

Tephritids   Family: Tephritidae

Mediterranean Fruit Fly   *Ceratitis capitata* **(Wiedemann)**

The adult fly is 5–6mm long, multicoloured (brown, black, white and yellow) with wings which have distinctive dark markings.

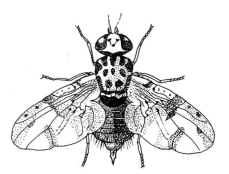

As the name suggests, this is not a native species. It is a serious pest of citrus fruits in the Mediterranean basin, Africa, Australia, South and Central America. Coffee beans, tomatoes, peaches, cherries, plums, apricots, pears and other tropical fruits are also attacked. The female lays her eggs under the skin of the fruit while on the plant and the larvae then bore inside. As many as twelve may

Mediterranean Fruit Fly –
Ceratitis capitata
(Wiedemann)

be present and their tunnels can cause bacteria and fungi to enter, resulting in decay.

The larvae are small, white, fragile worm-like creatures. When removed from the fruit, they quickly die and turn brown or black. The larvae are more frequently found in Ireland than the adults. The latter have occasionally been discovered in wholesalers, retailers and homes after emerging from recently imported fruit. The larvae do little damage except near the centre and most of the fruit remains edible.

If unnoticed these larvae may be swallowed by people. Adults appear to digest and kill them, but in small children, they have been known to pass alive through the intestine. Health inspectors find it difficult to detect infestations, as the samples are normally rotten when submitted for examination and the 'evidence' has disappeared. For this reason, if you find 'worms' in fruit and wish to have them identified, put them immediately into a convenient preservative such as whiskey, vodka or gin.

In Britain, other imported fruit flies have been recorded and it is probable that these also occur in Ireland but have been overlooked.

Lesser Dung Flies   Family: Sphaeroceridae

Sewage Fly   *Leptocera caenosa* **(Rondani)**

The adults are small (*c*. 4mm) black insects which can occur in enormous numbers and there may be thousands of specimens present in an infestation. They can be mistaken for fruit flies.

Sewage Fly –
Leptocera caenosa
(Rondani)

This species has been found breeding in modern sewage disposal tanks in Canada, and in Britain it is often associated with cracked pipes, where the larvae feed on sewage seeping into the soil. It has been so abundant in water-closets as to be a pest. The larvae have been reared in various organically rich substances, including horse and sheep manure.

Although only recently reported in Ireland, the sewage fly is potentially a serious health hazard because of its breeding habits. Usually the first indication of an infestation is the presence of numerous specimens crawling on the inside of windows. They can also be carried from one building to another in people's clothes. Adults could transfer disease organisms from breeding sites to patients in hospitals or to other people via contact with their food.

Because many past infestations of the sewage fly may have been dismissed as those of 'fruit flies' and their significance overlooked, the species is probably more common in this country than the present records indicate. To date, the species is known from several Irish localities ranging from Down to Cork. Incidents have been reported from a house, a maternity hospital, a windowless basement storehouse below a shop and an enclosed shopping centre. Infestations have been traced to a seepage of effluent from a blocked drain in a nearby premises, a drain containing milk solids and a blocked sewage drain. The adults are notorious for their ability to squeeze through very small openings, and two of the infestations in Ireland occurred when they entered buildings through cracks in the walls.

Shore Flies   Family: Ephydridae

Urinal Fly   *Teichomyza fusca* **Macquart**

This ephydrid fly is an obnoxious creature. The adults are small (5mm) brownish olive insects and the species has been recorded several times in Ireland. It can occur wherever there are cesspits or material soaked in human or animal urine. Although similar problems have not been yet reported in this country, abroad the larvae form dense masses blocking drains and septic tanks. In addition, the immature stages may be accidentally ingested in foul water, resulting in myiasis (see page 153).

Adult

Urinal Fly –
Teichomyza fusca
Macquart

Larva

Seaweed Flies   Family: Coelopidae

Seaweed Fly   *Coelopa frigida* **(Fabricius)**

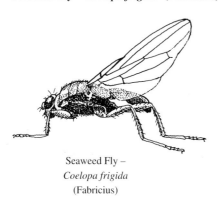

Seaweed Fly –
Coelopa frigida
(Fabricius)

The adults are small to medium-sized (4–12mm), bristly and flattened flies which are present throughout the year, often in large swarms.

The whole life-cycle of this widely distributed species is associated with the banks of rotting seaweed found on some Irish beaches above the high-tide mark. The larvae live on the moist vegetable material inside. Occasionally they accidentally enter nearby houses, garages and other buildings. However, since the flies are very attracted to certain chemicals including trichloroethylene, they may deliberately seek out premises containing these substances.

The swarms have a habit of settling on any beach object and if adults come indoors after resting on garbage, faeces or other noxious materials, they can be a health hazard, especially on food.

Sunbathers, picnickers and other users of beaches are often highly irritated by these insects, but they are a valuable source of nutrition for shore-birds.

Moth Flies   Family: Psychodidae

The owl midges or hairy moth flies are easily recognisable. They are minute (*c.* 5mm) midge-like flies with ovate and pointed wings covered with scales and hairs.

There are sixty species in Ireland and they mainly live in aquatic habitats but development can take place in cow-dung, other excrement, wet and decaying matter, including grass clippings. Around buildings, they are usually associated with drains. Indoors, they may frequent toilets, including urinals in public houses and sinks in domestic dwellings, where the larvae live in the moist bacterial scum that accumulates in downpipes or overflow channels. The adults may accidentally enter buildings where they may be seen running actively on windows.

Adult

Moth Fly –
Psychodidae

Larva

They have a curious, jerky gait but can also remain perfectly still. Moth flies neither bite nor sting and generally only cause annoyance, sometimes by flying across the eye line.

Black Fungus Gnats   Family: Sciaridae

The black fungus gnats or sciarids found in buildings are small (*c.* 4mm) black flies. Their flight appears slow and aimless and it can be irritating when they fly past computer screens or repeatedly distract the eye of a person relaxing in front of the television or reading a book.

We have not found many males in populations of the commonest indoor species, suggesting that some species are parthenogenetic or predominantly parthenogenetic (in other words, the females can reproduce without males).

The group breeds in situations containing decaying plant material, in animal excrement and in rotten wood attacked by fungi. Indoors, adults are frequently seen around potted plants where the

91

larvae can be very abundant in the soil or in any decaying plant matter, particularly if a bulb has gone off. This habitat is the source of most infestations in Ireland. The most exotic breeding medium we have heard of was medieval leather. In Britain, they seemed to be also feeding in decaying peat used as an insulating layer in old-fashioned steel safes. Some species damage plants in greenhouses and mushroom houses in Ireland.

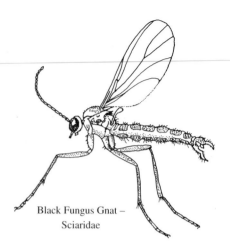

Black Fungus Gnat –
Sciaridae

Bibionids   Family: Bibionidae

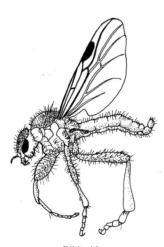

Bibionid –
Bibionidae

Many bibionids are conspicuous hairy black flies with the commonest species ranging in size from 3.5 to 12mm. The larvae feed on roots and decaying organic matter in the soil while the adults can be useful pollinators. Artificial fly imitations of bibionids are very popular with Irish anglers.

At certain times of year, the adults emerge in large numbers and may accidentally enter premises. They may also cause concern by resting in their hundreds on outside walls or on sheets on clothes-lines. However, they are completely harmless. We heard of an incident in Northern Ireland, where bibionids were accused of having bitten people while swarming on lawns, but it turned out to be a misunderstanding: the problem was actually caused by bird fleas.

Because of their abundance, they have several popular names including St Mark's fly, the hawthorn and blossom or fever fly. The latter is a misnomer as these insects do not transmit any human disease.

Daddy-Long-Legs   Family: Tipulidae

Daddy-long-legs or craneflies vary greatly in size, but some are very large insects reaching 65mm. The adults have slender bodies with long dangling legs. Those most commonly found are various different species of the large genus *Tipula*.

In summer or autumn, they may be a nuisance when they are attracted indoors by lights through open windows or doors. Clumsy fliers, they may scare people, particularly children, by bumbling about a room or knocking into light-shades. However, they cause no damage indoors and are completely harmless.

The larvae of the commonest species, known as leatherjackets, live just under the soil and feed on the roots of plants. Large numbers may cause bare patches in lawns. They have also been found in

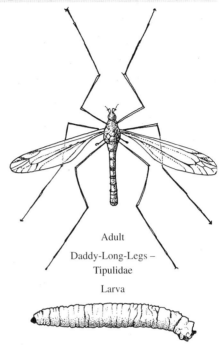

Adult
Daddy-Long-Legs –
Tipulidae

Larva

thatch. In the Dublin area, a species with flightless females is abundant in the autumn. The females often crawl up the outside walls of premises and have caused concern to householders.

Winter Gnats   Family: Trichoceridae

Resembling small craneflies, these distinctive gnats are among the commonest insects in winter and are a very important source of food for birds at that time of year.

All belong to the single genus *Trichocera* which includes several similar species. On fine days, the adults form large swarms, and watching the delicate adults dancing in sunbeams is one of winter's pleasures. The larvae live in decaying vegetable matter such as rotting leaves. They have been known to damage stored potatoes. During the winter, if windows are left open, large numbers of adults may be attracted indoors but they are harmless and do not bite.

Winter Gnat –
Trichocera sp

93

Window Gnats   Family: Anisopodidae

There are a few Irish species, belonging to the genus *Sylvicola*, which frequently enter houses and can be easily recognised by their characteristically marked wings. Adults often rest on vertical surfaces (such as walls or windows) and when disturbed, they have a jerky erratic flight.

Window Gnat –
Sylvicola sp

They can be attracted to fermenting substances such as decaying fruit or home-brewed wine. Window gnats may breed in such situations and in kitchen debris or soiled and neglected dishcloths if adequate hygiene precautions are not taken. In general, the larvae feed on decaying matter with a high organic content. This includes dung, sewage, other animal products and fermenting materials containing yeasts.

In Britain, window gnats have been responsible for cases of urogenital myiasis.

Mosquitoes   Family: Culicidae

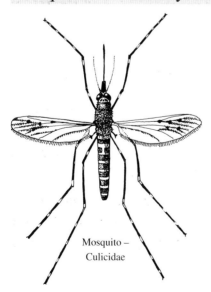

Mosquito –
Culicidae

There are eighteen species in Ireland, a fact which surprises many people. Resembling small (up to 6mm) craneflies, the females have a long projecting proboscis used for sucking blood. Luckily, most Irish mosquitoes are completely harmless, only feeding on frogs, rodents, farm animals and birds. However, a few species cause major health and nuisance problems here by biting humans.

Banded Mosquito *Culiseta annulata* (Schrank)

The banded mosquito is one notorious biter which enters houses. The species is widespread, the young living in drains, saltmarshes, freshwater pools and other standing water. It can even thrive in rain-filled kitchen utensils abandoned in the garden. Frequently, adults hibernate indoors where they occasionally attack the human residents. The bite can be highly irritating and may result in a severe allergic reaction. In some Dublin areas, susceptible people have had to move house to escape a persistent mosquito problem.

Common Gnat *Culex pipiens* Linnaeus

A smaller species, the common gnat, regularly comes indoors to hibernate and may be noticed resting on ceilings. The females are harmless and do not bite humans as our blood is unpalatable to them. However, a variety of this species (from *molestus*) is a vicious man-biter.

Anophelines *Anopheles* spp

The anopheline mosquitoes are capable of transmitting malaria. In England, people have contracted this disease without travelling abroad. It is believed that they were bitten by infective insects escaping from intercontinental aircraft at nearby airports.

Although we are unaware of any similar cases in Ireland, the possibility does exist. It should be remembered that malaria did exist in this country. At the time of the Crimean war, returning soldiers introduced the disease into mosquitoes in the Cork area and it persisted there for many years, affecting local people.

Biting Midges or Ceratopogonids   Family: Ceratopogonidae

Only one group of these insects (*Culicoides* spp) attacks mammals in Ireland. The adults are minute insects, rarely exceeding 5mm, and are popularly known as 'no-see-ums' because they normally escape our attention until we are bitten. Only the females have piercing mouth parts which are adapted for cutting wounds into the skins of their hosts and for sucking up blood.

People vary in their susceptibility to midges—some in a group will be severely affected while others will be virtually ignored. The bites are highly irritating and any exposed parts of the body will be attacked. Many humans have intense allergic reactions to them, often developing itchy lumps which can become infected if scratched.

95

The biting species are widely distributed throughout the country, but some vicious ones are very abundant in scenic areas, particularly boggy mountainous regions. Parts of Wicklow, the south-west, west and north-west are notorious for these pests. In one incident on Lower Lough Bray in Co Wicklow, we witnessed tourists and anglers 'running for their lives' to escape the attentions of ceratopogonids.

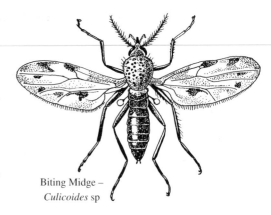

Biting Midge – *Culicoides* sp

The adults are poor fliers and are most active on warm, sultry, windless days. They can swarm in incredible numbers on suitable evenings, greatly inhibiting human outdoor pursuits. They will also readily enter buildings to attack the inhabitants if windows or doors are left open.

The larvae are aquatic or semi-aquatic, living in mud or at the surface of ponds, ditches, and so on. They can also occur in farmyard litter heaps, compost heaps in gardens and similar situations.

Non-Biting Midges or Chironomids   Family: Chironomidae

Chironomids are a large group of Irish insects, with over three hundred and fifty known species. They are delicate gnat-like flies (1–10mm long). The males gather together in large dancing swarms in sheltered places.

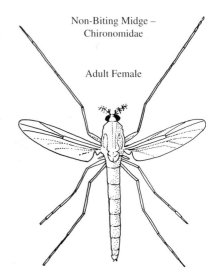

Non-Biting Midge – Chironomidae

Adult Female

The larvae are mainly aquatic, but some species prefer terrestrial habitats including decaying vegetable matter. The larvae of some species are bright red and are known as bloodworms. They can occur in huge numbers in polluted waters. The adults may cause nuisance problems, particularly near polluted lakes and rivers, by entering nearby houses and other premises in large numbers when attracted by lights at night. Chironomids do not bite humans, but in high concentrations the adults may provoke allergic reactions.

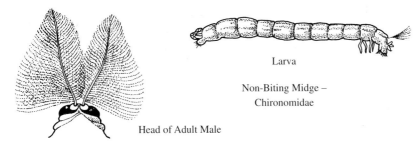

Larva

Non-Biting Midge –
Chironomidae

Head of Adult Male

Water-Mains Midge   *Paratanytarsus grimmi* (Schneider)

The adults are small green flies. The larvae are red–green, with a small brown head. When mature, they reach 3–4mm. The normal habitat is shallow standing water, where it lives among vegetation. In Britain, there are records from garden ponds and indoor aquaria as well as water-mains.

There are no males and the females can produce the next generation by themselves (parthenogenesis). Within the confines of the water-mains, the larva changes into a pupa in which the adult develops. Since it is impossible for the female to emerge inside a water-filled pipe, she lays her eggs within the pupal skin, which then ruptures. The eggs are thus released and the cycle recommences.

Although only recently discovered in Ireland in water-mains in the north-west, we have long suspected that this species was responsible for reports of 'worms' in drinking water here. Since the water-mains midge has the ability to live generation after generation inside pipes, occasional specimens emerge from taps. If noticed, their presence may disgust consumers. During 1973, one British water company experienced 1642 complaints from customers concerning this insect alone. We are unaware of any health risk, but discovery of any of its stages in drinking water does affect customer confidence in treatment procedures and general cleanliness of the water.

Chapter 6: Butterflies and Moths— Order: Lepidoptera

...you would be another Penelope;

yet they say all the yarn she spun in Ulysses' absence

did but fill Ithaca full of moths.

William Shakespeare, *Coriolanus* Act 1, Sc. III

Cabbage White Butterflies   Family: Pieridae

Three species of these butterflies attack cabbage and other brassicas in Ireland, but only the following two are important pests.

Large White (or Cabbage White) Butterfly *Pieris brassicae* **(Linnaeus)**

This insect can reach 63.5mm in size. These insects are outdoor pests only, but when various brassicas are brought indoors the caterpillars are frequently discovered on cabbage, lettuce or products prepared from these vegetables. The larva of the large white is hairy with a black head. Reaching 41mm in length, the general colour is greyish green with three longitudinal yellow stripes and black blotches.

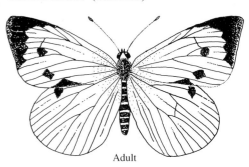

Adult

Large White Butterfly –
Pieris brassicae
(Linnaeus)

Caterpillar

Small White Butterfly *Pieris rapae* **(Linnaeus)**

The caterpillar is smaller (25mm) than that of the large white, and predominantly pale green. A light greenish yellow, narrow line extends along its back.

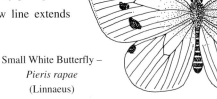

Small White Butterfly –
Pieris rapae
(Linnaeus)

House-Moths   Family: Oecophoridae

Brown House-Moth *Hoffmannophila pseudospretella* **(Stainton)**

The large (15–22mm) adult is bronze–brown in colour with dark brown to black flecks on its fore-wings. The hind-wings are a shining brownish grey. The body of the caterpillar is white while the head is brown and when mature reaches a length of about 16mm.

This species is one of the commonest pests in Ireland, being widespread both in the wild and indoors. The adults are good fliers and will often enter houses and other buildings at night through open windows and doors. However, some infestations are traceable to birds' nests.

The female can lay five to six hundred eggs. The caterpillars eat stored cereals, dried fruit, seeds, fabrics, furs and other materials of animal or vegetable origin. The species often occurs in domestic premises, destroying clothes and furnishings. 'Moth-proofed' synthetic carpets may be holed by mature larvae making pupation chambers. Specimens can live on the dust and debris between floorboards and behind skirting boards. In Irish warehouses, mills, granaries and shops, the species can be a serious pest, damaging stored commodities including

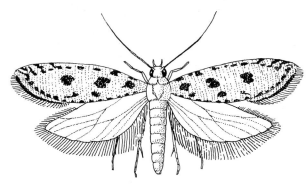

Brown House-Moth –
Hoffmannophila pseudospretella
(Stainton)

bulk wheat and bagged flour. It also attacks the corks of wine-bottles stored in damp cellars and insect collections in this country.

The growing larvae thrive in the high humidity which is so common in Ireland. Often the first indication of an infestation is when the newly emerged adults are noticed sitting on walls or ceilings. Upon discovery, the adult is adept at escaping from the wrath of the house-holder, dropping into crevices, behind cupboards and other objects to wait until the coast is once again clear. Although the adults have no biting mouth parts and are unable to feed, they can sometimes squeeze into poorly sealed containers or packages and lay their eggs inside with devastating results. In one Dublin house, for example, several hundred moths emerged from a partially opened, large box of dog pellets which the dog disliked. These had been stored on the top of a kitchen cupboard and then forgotten about until the infestation was noticed. Caterpillars have been observed happily eating window displays in shops on Dublin's fashionable Grafton Street! In Co Cork, larvae were found in books stored in an archive. In the same county, the species was common in excrement which builders had left in an attic. In Co Donegal, a person complained of abdominal pain and a larva was found alive in the vomit. It was claimed that the specimen was vomited but this is considered unlikely.

White-Shouldered House-Moth   *Endrosis sarcitrella* (Linnaeus)

The white-shouldered house-moth is not as serious a pest as the brown house-moth, but it is widespread in Ireland and will also readily fly indoors. The adult is recognisable by its white head and thorax which contrast with the silvery grey fore-wings marked by dark almost black patches— hence the popular name. It can reach 11mm in length.

The caterpillar resembles that of the brown house-moth but is dull white in colour and smaller (14mm). The species is a general feeder and scavenger, being common in warehouses, granaries, farm-buildings and houses. Its diet is similar to that of the brown house-moth. Interesting Irish records

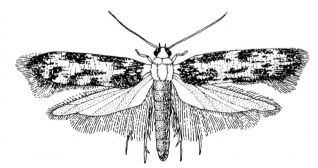

White-Shouldered House-Moth –
Endrosis sarcitrella
(Linnaeus)

include a larva in a tea bag, a live larva on a dinner plate along with cooked sausage rolls and larvae in custard powder.

Clothes Moths   Family: Tineidae

There are a number of species which can cause problems in the home and which attack a variety of manufactured goods, especially textiles.

Common Clothes Moth   *Tineola bisselliella* **(Hummel)**

The adult is uniformly golden or yellowish grey in colour, reaching 8mm in length.

The larvae feed on all materials, clothes and textiles of animal origin including woollens, furs and carpets. Drugs containing albumin and dried meat extracts may be attacked. The species will also live on the felted fluff which accumulates in the cold-air ducts of central heating systems. As many as a hundred eggs may be laid. The larva spins a fine tube around itself as a protection. This tube is fixed and becomes covered with the remains of the food and pellets of excrement which is the same colour as the food. Being round, the pellets may be mistaken for eggs. The caterpillar is creamy white with a golden brown head.

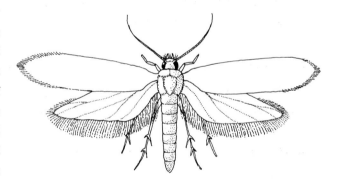

Common Clothes Moth –
Tineola bisselliella
(Hummel)

In Britain, the common clothes moth was a most serious pest but seems to have declined in recent years due to chemicals, man-made fibres and vacuum cleaners. Surprisingly, the species has never been common in Ireland and there are very few records. The earliest is 1855 from houses in Dublin. In the 1940s, it was reported as being widespread in Belfast but in very small numbers. Subsequently, a serious infestation occurred in a textile collection in a museum. Recent Irish

101

records (all from Dublin) include adults found indoors in photographic fluid, infesting a clothing store and eating red fox furs in a warehouse.

Case-Bearing Clothes Moth *Tinea pellionella* (Linnaeus)

This species is very similar to the common clothes moth. However, the adult may be distinguished by its dusty brown colour and three dark spots on the fore-wing. In addition, the caterpillar spins a tubular case which becomes covered with fragments of food including wool (clothes, carpets, curtains), fur or feathers. Unlike the common clothes moth, this case is portable and used for protection—it can even be carried up vertical walls.

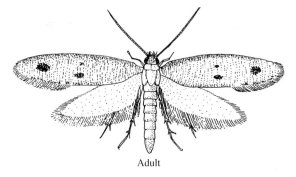

Adult

Case-Bearing Clothes Moth –
Tinea pellionella
(Linnaeus)

Caterpillar

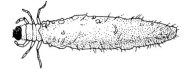

In the early stages of infestations, the young larvae are very small and therefore very difficult to detect. They are usually only noticed after some damage has taken place, in other words, when holes or bare patches appear in the fabric and accumulations of larval excrement become obvious. Infestations can arise from birds' nests.

In 1941, this species was considered to be probably abundant in houses all over the country but now appears to be rare. There are modern records from Dublin and Monaghan. These include larvae found in an Ethiopian wall tapestry, and a carpet infestation. Other species of case-bearing clothes moths have been found in Britain and they may yet turn up in Ireland.

Large Pale Clothes Moth *Tinea pallescentella* Stainton

The adult is large (19mm) and brownish. The caterpillar's body is white and the head is brown. When mature, the larvae grow to 7–12mm. Like most other species in this family, a non-transportable larval tube is constructed for protection and covered with remains from the food material and excrement.

Large Pale Clothes Moth –
Tinea pallescentella
Stainton

This species attacks a variety of materials of animal origin including wool, hair, feathers, fur and hides. Woollen fabrics are normally eaten under damp conditions. In Ireland, the species is widely distributed outdoors and in nature plays an important role in recycling the remains in bird and wasp nests as well as animal corpses. In one Dublin house recently, large numbers of larvae were feeding on a woollen carpet, especially under a coal scuttle and a couch which were infrequently moved and providing a suitably dark environment.

Corn Moth *Nemapogon granella* **(Linnaeus)**

The adult is creamy white in colour with brown patches on the fore-wings. Its wing span is 10–14mm. The body of the larva is white or yellowish white with a brown head. The species mainly attacks rye and less often wheat. In Britain, it is considered a minor pest. There are few Irish records although in the 1940s, it was considered to be probably common in granaries here. There are definite records from a Derry granary and three Belfast mills but in low numbers. The species was plentiful in one infestation where it was breeding in spillage. In Cork city, it is still common in The Maltings.

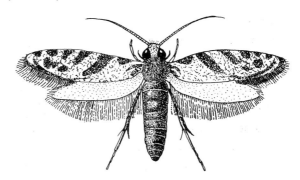

Corn Moth –
Nemapogon granella
(Linnaeus)

Pyralid Moths   Family: Pyralidae

Pyralid larvae have distinct black or brown spots (pinacula) on the body giving them a spotted appearance, whereas the other moth families covered here do not.

103

Mediterranean Flour Moth   *Ephestia kuehniella* Zeller

Also popularly known as the mill moth, the adults have pale grey or brownish grey forewings with darker markings. The wing span is 20–25mm. The larvae are pinkish or yellowish white with a chestnut-brown head. Maturity (15–19mm) can be reached in six weeks and there may be three to five generations each year.

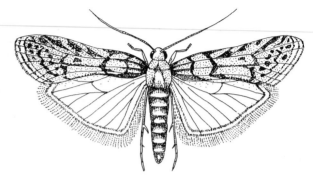

Mediterranean Flour Moth –
Ephestia kuehniella
Zeller

This is a very troublesome flour-mill pest in these islands. The species was probably first introduced about 1887 and it mainly attacks wheat-flour. However, other meal and flour, cereals (oatmeal, rice, maize) and their products (pasta, biscuits, cakes), nuts and other vegetable products and even dried insects will be eaten. Although the larvae only consume small quantities of food, in large numbers they cause extensive fouling of the foodstuff with excrement. In addition, they spin silken webbing amongst the food and this may cause matting, resulting in the clogging of machinery, elevators and chutes. Heavy infestation causes 'souring' of grain and flour. In Ireland, this flour moth is practically confined to mills and bakeries, and does not thrive in unheated premises. Recent records include bakeries in Dublin but it has also been found in a crisp factory and in imported French grain. In houses, it has been found in purchased buckwheat and oat flakes. In Waterford, it was discovered in breakfast cereal. One larva was even found baked in a slice of bread.

Warehouse Moth   *Ephestia elutella* (Hübner)

Other popular names are the cacao moth or the stored tobacco moth. The adult may be distinguished from the Mediterranean flour moth by its smaller size (14–20mm) and by the forewings, which are paler in colour and have oblique cross lines and a conspicuous pale line.

The larvae feed on a wide range of raw materials and finished products, including cocoa beans and manufactured chocolate, dried fruit, nuts, pulses, oilseeds and oilcakes, grains, grain products and tobacco. They only consume small quantities of food but cause extensive fouling with excrement and silken webbing. Huge populations can build up.

This moth is widely distributed in temperate parts of the world, particularly in Britain where it a common pest. It is mainly found in the protected environment of warehouses, factories and stores. The species has often been imported into Ireland in commodities and B. P. Beirne reported that in the 1940s a large consignment of cocoa beans was so heavily infested that it was unfit for the manufacture of

Adult

Warehouse Moth –
Ephestia elutella
(Hübner)

Caterpillar

chocolate. It does not seem to be a serious pest here now. However, live and dead larvae ('worms') or adults have been found in purchased chocolate goods. Such infections can occur in the factory or the shop, for the female moth can crawl through the slightest gap in the wrapping of a package and lay her eggs. In 1989, a larva was discovered in breakfast muesli by a householder in Galway.

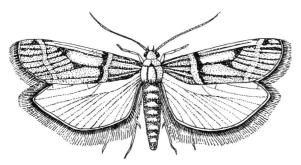

Tropical Warehouse Moth –
Ephestia cautella
(Walker)

Tropical Warehouse Moth
Ephestia cautella (Walker)

Also known as the dried currant moth, this species closely resembles the warehouse moth and can only be identified by examining the genitalia of the adults. Its diet is also similar. As the name signifies, the species is tropical in origin but it is frequently introduced by shipping into these islands. All stages of the life-cycle may be found throughout the year in heated premises.

European Corn Borer   *Ostrinia nubilalis* (Hübner)

Adults are brownish red with yellow markings on the wings, a body length of 12–14mm and wingspan of 29–37mm. The larva is pale yellow in colour and covered with many dark spotted areas, reaching 28mm in length.

This species is an important agricultural pest of maize (sweetcorn) and other plants including hops. It is known from most of continental Europe, south-east England, north Africa,

European Corn Borer –
Ostrinia nubilalis
(Hübner)

the Middle East, the eastern United States and southern Canada. There is one record of an adult moth from Ireland which is almost certainly a migrant from southern England or continental Europe. Dead caterpillars, blanched white, are sometimes imported in canned sweetcorn and tomatoes. It could also occur in fresh or frozen sweetcorn but we have not encountered any such cases.

Indian Meal Moth   *Plodia interpunctella* (Hübner)

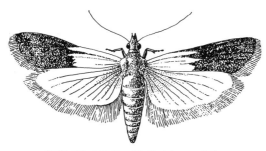

Indian Meal Moth – *Plodia interpunctella*
(Hübner)

The fore-wing of the adult is reddish yellow with the outer half varying in colour from light purplish red to dark purplish black. The wingspan varies from 14–20mm. The larva is yellowish white, pinkish or greenish with a yellowish brown head which is usually marked underneath with dark brown.

This species attacks a wide variety of foodstuffs, particularly those of vegetable origin. The known diet includes stored grain and its products, dried fruit and nuts as well as oilseeds and oilcake, soya beans, cocoa beans, chocolate, spices, pulses and even drugs. The larva can survive on any dry manufactured by-products of any or a combination of any of the above foods. It becomes fully grown in from two weeks to two years, fouling the foodstuffs with frass (excrement) and the silken web which it spins.

The Indian meal moth thrives in warm climates and is very common in tropical and sub-tropical regions. It was first noted in these islands in 1847 and is continually being reintroduced through imports. It is now considered to be widespread in warehouses here and in Britain.

Small Magpie Moth *Eurrhypara hortulata* (Linnaeus)

The adult is a large (30–35mm) white moth speckled with black markings. The caterpillar is yellowish with two dark dots at the front of the body and a dark band along the back. The head is brown.

This species is widely distributed in Europe and common throughout Ireland. From August to September, the caterpillar feeds mostly on nettles but occasionally on mint or other plants. It lives within rolled and spun leaves. When fully grown in the autumn, it leaves the food plant to look for a hibernation site. At this time, specimens can enter houses or other buildings, particularly when nettles are growing

Small Magpie Moth –
Eurrhypara hortulata
(Linnaeus)

on adjacent waste ground. They can occur in large numbers, crawling up walls and hanging from curtains, but have not been known to cause any damage. In one Irish incident, they contaminated antiseptic cream in a factory and it is possible that they cause similar problems for other manufacturers here.

Ctenuchids   Family: Ctenuchidae

Banana Moths *Antichloris* **spp**

The adult moths are beautifully coloured—dark indigo, yellow and red.

The larvae, pupae and adults of these exotic species are sometimes imported with bananas from South and Central American countries. Several species are now recorded in Britain and Ireland. They occasionally emerge indoors in houses and warehouses. One would not expect these species to occur outdoors in these islands, but in 1982, an adult came to a lighted window in Aberdeen, Scotland. There are Irish records of two species. Live adults were collected in a fruit merchant's store, the Dublin Fruit and Vegetable Market and the stores department of a mental hospital.

Tortrix Moths   Family: Tortricidae

Codling Moth *Cydia pomonella* **(Linnaeus)**

The caterpillars of this moth are pale pink, with a few scattered setae and a brown head.

They eat into the flesh of maturing apples, making them inedible. Pears and other fruits are also attacked. Specimens can be brought indoors in infested fruit and these 'worms', which may be 20mm in length, can be discovered while eating the fruit. In a house in Clontarf, Co Dublin, a caterpillar was found under the covering of a mattress of a bedroom

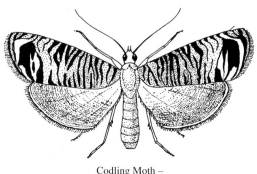

Codling Moth –
Cydia pomonella
(Linnaeus)

which had been used for storing apples. Infested fruit may be spotted, before eating, by checking the skin for a hole, usually near the stalk or opposite end—this hole may be covered by brown frass (excrement).

Noctuids   Family: Noctuidae

Cabbage Moth *Mamestra brassicae* **Linnaeus**

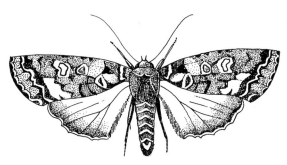

Cabbage Moth –
Mamestra brassicae
Linnaeus

The caterpillar has a pale yellowish brown or dark brown head. The body varies from brown to greyish green, paler below. There is a dark brown line along the back and a pale spot on each segment.

Like cabbage white butterflies, this species attacks brassicas (cabbage, lettuce, cauliflower, sprouts) and is widespread and fairly common. It also eats other plants including beetroot, peas, potato, tomato, rhubarb and onion. Specimens occasionally occur in fresh, frozen or processed vegetables or salads containing lettuce.

Tomato Worm *Heliothis armigera* **(Hübner)**

The caterpillar has a yellowish head marked with brown. The body varies from brown to green and is rough to the touch due to small spines. There are white and brown longitudinal bands along the body. Fully grown, it is about 40mm long. The adult is a brown moth with a wingspan of the

Adult
Tomato Worm –
Heliothis armigera
(Hübner)

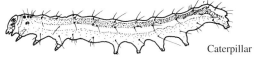

Caterpillar

same size. In the warmer parts of the old world, this species attacks a wide range of crops but it is not native to Ireland. In southern Europe it is mainly a pest of tomato and maize. The larvae feed on leaves, buds, flowers and fruit of the host plant and may be imported alive on fresh tomatoes, peppers and maize. Dead larvae are occasionally found in canned tomatoes. Specimens could also occur in other host vegetables—canned or frozen.

Hawk-Moths   Family: Sphingidae

Death's-Head Hawk-Moth   *Acherontia atropos* Linnaeus

The adult is a very large (130mm) distinctive-looking moth with brown fore-wings and yellow hind-wings marked with brown bands. The abdomen is yellow and brown. The markings on the thorax resemble a skull—hence the popular name. The caterpillar is also huge (130mm) and is very variable in colour with brown, yellowish and green forms. Although caterpillars elsewhere in Europe are mainly of the yellowish form, in our experience most of those found in Ireland are brownish black, marked with brown bands and streaks. The body ends in a tail.

The adult is an occasional migrant to Ireland usually in the autumn from its native Africa, but it has arrived earlier. Sometimes, this species can be a pest, because it takes honey from bee hives; for this reason it is also known here as the 'bee robber'. It can emit a shrill squeak. A specimen sent to the Natural History Museum was, according to the accompanying letter, killed indoors by children while it was hiding in a coat hanging on a door. They heard it squeaking and thought that the moth was a mouse.

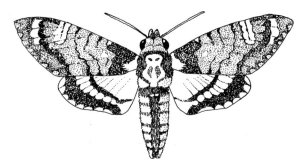

Death's-Head Hawk-Moth –
Acherontia atropos
Linnaeus

In this country, the caterpillars feed mainly on potato but they will feed on other plants including garden privet. There are several Irish records of live individuals being discovered indoors in fresh vegetables, but they do not cause any harm.

Chapter 7: Ants, Bees and Wasps — Order: Hymenoptera

The ant has made himself illustrious

Through constant industry industrious.

So what?

Would you be calm and placid

If you were full of formic acid?

Ogden Nash[6]

Ants, bees and wasps are familiar to most people because of their close association with humans. Many are social insects which live in nests and work together as a community. Each individual nest is ruled by a queen, though sometimes there may be two or more queens. The queen controls small to large numbers of sterile female workers who carry out most of the various tasks necessary for the survival and well-being of the community. In addition, there are usually a few fertile males which are reluctantly tolerated. After mating with the next generation of queens, the males die. Workers are most commonly seen but queens or males are sometimes encountered.

Other Hymenoptera, including some species of bee and wasp, are solitary (as are most insects) and only come together for reproduction. Many of the solitary wasps are internal parasites of other insect species. As a result they are beneficial to humanity by controlling the populations of various pests, including greenfly and wood-boring beetles.

Ants   Family: Formicidae

Some twenty species of ant occur in Ireland but only the native common black ant and a few exotic ones cause problems indoors. All the Irish ants are social insects and live in nests. In summer or early autumn, flying swarms may be obvious. These consist of mating males and females. The males soon die and each fertilised female or (potential) queen attempts to establish a new colony. If a suitable nest site is found, she sheds her wings and lays unfertilised eggs which develop into the

6 Zoo 1987, Stewart, Tabori & Chang, New York

sterile worker ants; and if conditions are suitable, she lays fertilised eggs, which develop into males and females (new queens).

One of the duties of the workers is to search for food. As a result, they are often noticed by householders when they come indoors. Three of the species described below are not native to Ireland but have arrived as a result of world trade. It is very likely that other harmful exotic ant species will become established here.

Common Black Ant   *Lasius niger* (Linnaeus)

- **Worker:** *c.* 3.5–5.0mm long, brown to brownish black and with no wings

- **Queen:** 8.0–9.0mm long, brownish black and with transparent wings which are only present for a few days

- **Male:** 3.5–5.0mm long, brownish black and with transparent wings

The common black ant is the species which is most frequently encountered indoors or outdoors. It is wonderfully well adapted to life in a variety of habitats, which explains its great success. Each nest contains a single queen and between several hundred and ten thousand workers. The workers kill flies and other small insects for the nest, take nectar from flowers and collect seeds.

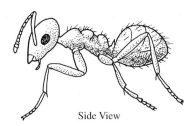

Side View

Common Black Ant –
Lasius niger
(Linnaeus)

Dorsal View

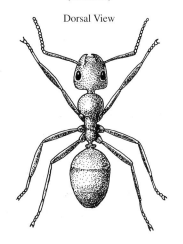

It is a very common species in urban areas where it nests under pavements, concrete, rocks and flagstones, in walls, tree stumps and under lawns. In rural areas, it occurs in sandy areas, in woodland, pasture and heath. These habitats may be cultivated or uncultivated, shady or exposed and range from the seashore to an altitude of at least 300 metres (1000 feet). In some modern houses, where concrete floors are laid on the ground floor, ants can travel underneath and appear indoors through cracks in the floor. They may also nest in the insulation layer of walls and visit kitchens and other areas at any time via breaks in the concrete or brickwork. Ants have preferences for particular soil types and they are scarce or absent from unsuitable ones.

The common black ant is an aggressive species and will attack other ants. This species does not actually sting, but it can squirt formic acid which, in contact with the skin, may cause a burning sensation.

Outdoors, people can be annoyed, while picnicking, by workers searching for food. When a worker locates a good source of food, it lays down a scent trail and then informs other ants in the nest. They follow the scent and within a relatively short time, there can be numerous ants travelling back and forth. When this happens indoors, it can cause problems for the householder. The food source may be a bowl of sugar, pot of jam or some other food (often sweet) in the larder or on the kitchen table. The removal of such items from a trail usually causes intense confusion amongst the workers.

Often the common black ant remains unnoticed until it swarms. On hot thundery days in late summer and early autumn (particularly from mid-August to early September), people are amazed to see thousands of winged ants emerging from manicured suburban gardens, grassy areas in public gardens and even from cracks in the pavement (for example, Merrion Square in Dublin). In some years the swarms are enormous and ants begin emerging on the same day over very large districts (all of urban Dublin, for example). Both males and females are present, for this is their nuptial or 'wedding' flight.

Pharaoh's Ant *Monomorium pharaonis* **(Linnaeus)**

- **Worker:** 2.0–2.4mm long, reddish yellow and with no wings

- **Queen:** 3.6–4.8mm long, reddish yellow and with wings when sexually active

- **Male:** 3.0mm long, black with yellow appendages (legs and antennae) and with transparent wings

The popular name for this ant is an indication of how long it has been associated with humans. The species is not native to Ireland, arriving here from the tropics. Through commerce, it was widely dispersed throughout the world, probably reaching Europe in the early part of the nineteenth century. The first British record occurred in 1828 and it was discovered in Ireland in the 1840s at Aghadoe Church, Co Wicklow. It is now an established pest and, in addition to Wicklow, has been found in counties Cork, Donegal and Dublin.

Pharaoh's ant has not lost its association with warm environments and it is only found in heated premises in Ireland. The species can cause massive infestations in such affected premises as bakeries, hotels (including bedrooms), restaurants, laundries, hospitals, public buildings, shops, blocks of flats and even houses. Workers and queens forage for food in long trails and they are strongly attracted to meat and fatty foods as well as sweet substances. They will also feed on other foods including less savoury items such as dead animals (rats and mice), rodent droppings and insects. The nests are usually located in warm, dark places with a high temperature ideally in the range 27°–30°C and a high relative humidity. There are interesting instances of this species living in the crevices of a bamboo plant in a hothouse at the National Botanic Gardens and under a fish tank in a tropical house of the Zoological Gardens. It can be transferred to domestic dwellings which are centrally heated.

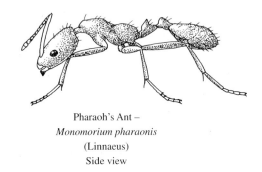

Pharaoh's Ant –
Monomorium pharaonis
(Linnaeus)
Side view

It is difficult or impossible to trace and eradicate some nests because of their inaccessible locations in places like the cavity spaces in walls, under floors, around hot water pipes, behind large ovens or in the foundations. Unlike most ants there may be several queens in a colony and once an infestation has become established in a building, satellite colonies are formed. These co-exist together as one big family consisting of hundreds of thousands to several million individuals. All stages of the life-cycle are found and produced throughout the year.

Pharaoh's ant is, potentially, a very serious health pest in hospitals, as it may transmit diseases between patients or wards. The disease organisms include *Clostridium*, *Pseudomonas*, *Salmonella*, *Staphylococcus* and *Streptococcus*. The ants can enter beds and get under the bandages covering patients' wounds. They have a habit of biting and stinging the eyelids and sensitive skin of infants. While searching for water, workers will visit such wet or moist substances as urine, faeces, drains, soiled bandages and bed pans. They wander widely and can enter the most unlikely equipment including syringes, 'sterile' dressings and packages. The ants may even be found in operating theatres, where their presence is a matter of grave concern.

Roger's Ant   *Hypoponera punctatissima* (Roger)

- **Worker:** 2.5–3.2mm long, reddish yellow to dark brown and wingless

- **Queen:** 3.5–3.8mm long, reddish yellow to dark brown; wings present in young queens but absent in older ones

- **Male:** 3.4–3.6mm long, reddish yellow to dark brown and wingless

Although it is widely distributed throughout Europe as well as tropical and subtropical areas, Roger's ant is almost certainly an introduced insect in Ireland. Specimens are sometimes imported in plant material from abroad, but the species is already established here. Infestations mainly occur in heated premises such as bakeries, factories, conservatories, greenhouses, kitchens, but colonies can exist outdoors in fermenting rubbish dumps and waste tips.

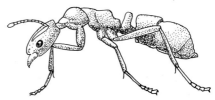

Roger's Ant –
Hypoponera punctatissima
(Roger)
Side View

Roger's ant is usually carnivorous, feeding on small insects and related creatures. This species causes problems in factories, particularly ones associated with the food industry. Each nest may contain large numbers of individuals and is normally in a very inaccessible place (such as under floors, cavities in walls, the empty space in cavity blocks) and extremely difficult to eradicate. The best method of locating the nest is to watch out for the swarming queens in July to September. These mate in the nest, the wingless males remaining inside. If the holes and cracks in bricks, floors and walls through which the queens escape are marked, they can be used to pinpoint the location of nests for fumigation.

Irish records include a tower block in central Belfast, the Custom House Dock and a suburban garden in Rathmines (both in Dublin), a mill at Bushmills, Co Antrim and a factory in Co Cavan.

Argentine Ant   *Iridomyrmex humilis* (Mayr)

- **Worker:** 2.2–2.8mm long, pale bronze to bronze black, wingless

- **Queen:** 4.5mm long, pale bronze to bronze black, with wings

- **Male:** 2.5–3.0mm long, bronze–black, with wings

Originating in South America, the Argentine ant has spread through trade, mainly in ships' cargoes, around the world. In Europe, particularly in the south and the Mediterranean region, it has become a well established and notorious pest. In Ireland, the species would only survive in permanently heated buildings and hothouses where it could nest in the masonry and woodwork. There may be several queens per colony and large interconnected colonies can develop since the workers from nearby nests will readily intermix.

Argentine Ant –
Iridomyrmex humilis
(Mayr)
Side View

The Argentine ant is aggressive, driving out other species. The workers actively forage for food at temperatures between 10°C and 30°C. Although preferring sweet substances, they will eat meat, including dead or alive insects.

The Argentine ant was first recorded in Ireland from a house in Belfast, Co Down, in July 1898 and the infestation lasted some five years. To eliminate the ants, it was necessary to dig to a depth of about 4 feet, where the nests were located, namely around the foundations and under the floor of the pantries, kitchen and sculleries. The ants did not come through the floor but instead appeared inside the walls and out of the framework of doors and windows. Workers are mainly active at night, being quieter between 2 and 8 pm. Although we have not found any other Irish records, unpublished cases are likely to have occurred. The species inhabits some British hospitals, where it spreads diseases. It is probable that it will eventually infest Irish hospitals.

Bees   Family: Apidae

Honey Bee   *Apis mellifera* **Linnaeus**

- **Worker:** 12mm

- **Queen:** *c.* 20mm

- **Male:** *c.*15mm

Honey Bee –
Apis mellifera
Linnaeus

The honey bee is the only insect that has been truly domesticated. The ancient Egyptians kept beehives 5000 years ago. Bees are valued as pollinators of various fruits and crops, as well as for their honey, but they can cause problems for householders mainly though swarming. Occasionally after a newly mated queen enters a hive, the old queen will leave, accompanied by a large number of workers. Such a swarm may settle on a house, forming a ball around her. At this stage, the bees in the swarm are very docile and will not sting. Local beekeepers are often anxious to collect such swarms so if you are troubled by one, contact a beekeeper near you, by checking the relevant regional telephone directory. Although they are not very aggressive, bees can sting and allergic people may require medical treatment (see Chapter 9 for additional information).

Mining Bee   *Andrena nigroaenea* **(Kirby)**

Mining Bee –
Andrena nigroaenea
(Kirby)

Resembling honey bees, mining bees are solitary nesters in the ground, although many nests may be together, giving an impression of communal life.

These bees are of economic importance, as they play a significant part in the fertilisation of the flowers of fruit trees in the spring months. This species has

117

rarely caused problems in Ireland, though a few years ago there was a population explosion of these bees in lawns in the Dublin area and householders were alarmed when the adult bees strayed indoors. However, they are harmless insects and the species has again become scarce.

Social Wasps   Family: Vespidae

These strikingly coloured black and yellow insects are familiar to everyone and are encountered by most people every year. There are six species in Ireland and the common wasp, which frequently nests in houses, is a typical example.

Common Wasp   *Vespula vulgaris* **(Linnaeus)**

- **Worker:** 10–15mm

- **Queen:** *c.* 20mm

- **Male:** *c.* 15mm

Wasp colonies are formed annually and the cycle begins when the hibernating queens, which are already mated from the previous autumn, wake up in the spring. Because they are so large, they are very obvious insects. Each one searches for a suitable nest site. Unfortunately, this is often in a house, particularly in the roofspace under the eaves.

Social Wasp –
Vespidae

Once the queen has selected a suitable place, she begins to construct the nest with paper made from wood scrapings and bound together with adhesive saliva. The first eggs are laid inside and when they hatch, the queen collects insects and other suitable food to feed the developing young. After about four weeks, the first sterile female workers emerge, taking over the role of gathering food. They also maintain and enlarge the nest and feed the young inside. From then on, the queen completely devotes herself to laying eggs, and wasp numbers rapidly increase. By the end of the summer, a successful colony can contain five to six thousand individuals, but between 25,000 and 30,000 wasps may have been reared.

In late summer or autumn, the queen lays fertile eggs, producing new queens and males, which mate. The new queens then hibernate through the winter, restarting the whole life-cycle in the spring.

Unlike bees, wasps do not store food for use in the winter. Consequently, the old queen and all the workers die off in the autumn and, at this time of year, nests are no longer a problem.

Workers are attracted to fruit, jam, soft drinks and similar sweet substances. They have painful stings and they can cause serious annoyance in houses, public houses or restaurants and on picnics. In years of great abundance, they have disrupted work in food factories.

Some people can become allergic to wasp venom, and this condition can be life-threatening. All stings should therefore be treated with great caution. (Advice on treatment is given in Chapter 9.)

Hornet *Vespa crabro* Linnaeus

- **Worker:** *c.* 20mm

- **Queen:** *c.* 30mm

- **Male:** *c.* 25mm

There are no hornets in Ireland, although people are often convinced that they have seen one. The usual culprit is the giant wood wasp. Hornets are similar to wasps, differing in their larger size and coloration. Instead of the distinctively contrasting yellow and black of wasps, hornets' bodies are yellow and brownish orange. In Britain, this species is mainly confined to south-eastern Wales and southern England and it is rarely encountered north of Sheffield.

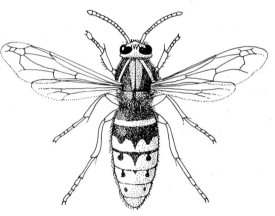

Hornet –
Vespa crabro
Linnaeus

119

Wood Wasps   Family: Siricidae

Giant Wood Wasp *Urocerus gigas* (**Linnaeus**)

Because of the large size (10–51mm) of the adult and its black and yellow colour, this species is often mistaken in Ireland for the hornet. The immature stages live in timber, particularly conifers. The life-cycle takes from two to three years to complete. The adults normally fly from June until early October and a loud buzzing sound may be made in flight.

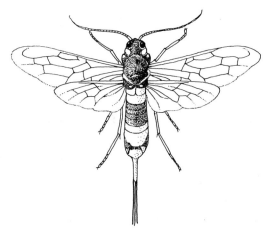

Giant Wood Wasp –
Urocerus gigas
(Linnaeus)

There are reports of families in the Wicklow mountains running 'for their lives', after mating swarms of giant wood wasps had congregated on picnic sites, but although the female has a long tail resembling a sting, this is only an ovipositor used for egg-laying in wood, and is neither a threat nor a danger to people.

The giant wood wasp is becoming commoner in Ireland because of the widespread planting of conifers. Although females only lay their eggs in living wood with bark, the whitish grub-like larvae may be present in harvested timber. As a result, adults sometimes emerge indoors from poorly seasoned wood (used for example in packing cases, pallets or even furniture), and the exit holes may cause damage. It is unlikely, however, that sufficient larvae would be present to cause structural damage.

Large blue woodwasps (for example *Sirex cyaneus* Fabricius and *Sirex noctilio* Fabricius) can emerge from imported furniture.

Parasitic Wasps   Several Families

The following three families include numerous parasitic wasps, but only three species are included here. These creatures are beneficial, controlling the numbers of other insects by parasitising them. Some have long ovipositors used for laying their eggs inside their hosts' bodies. If the ovipositor is mistaken for a sting, these wasps can cause alarm when found indoors, but they are harmless to human health.

Ichneumons   Family: Ichneumonidae

Wood Wasp Ichneumon *Rhyssa persuasoria* **(Linnaeus)**

This is a magnificent-looking creature, associated with the giant wood wasp and parasitic on its larvae. The adult is a large (up to 90mm, including ovipositor) black and white insect. The female has a very long ovipositor with which she drills through wood and lays her eggs on the young of the wood wasp. Feeding on the outside body surface of the host, the parasite takes some five weeks to mature. There is a resting stage before pupation and the adult does not emerge until the following spring.

Adults sometimes occur indoors, emerging from coniferous wood used as firewood, in building or to make furniture. Certain ichneumons are attracted to light and thus may enter houses. If handled, the females of some species may attempt to use their ovipositors as stings. One of these is the large red ichneumonid, *Ophion luteus* (Linnaeus), which is 11–20mm long.

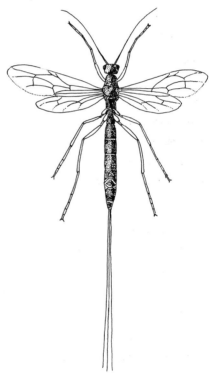

Wood Wasp Ichneumon –
Rhyssa persuasoria
(Linnaeus)

121

Chalcid Wasps   Family: Chalcididae

Woodworm Chalcid Wasp   *Theocolax formiciformis* Westwood

These chalcids are small (1.3–3.1mm), ant-like insects, blackish and normally wingless.

Although reported only from Donegal, Dublin and Mayo, this species is the commonest parasite in this country of furniture beetles or woodworm and probably occurs throughout the island. The adult lays her eggs on the woodworm or near by, in its tunnel, and when they hatch, the chalcid larvae suck out the body contents of their prey. When mature, the wasps can bore out through wood.

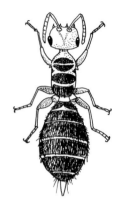

Woodworm Chalcid Wasp –
Theocolax formiciformis
Westwood

Braconid Wasps   Family: Braconidae

Woodworm Braconid Wasp   *Spathius exarator* (Linnaeus)

The adults vary greatly in size (3–7mm), their size being dependent on their woodworm host. The female has an ovipositor about the same length as her body. This species favours damp situations, such as cellars, where it is easier to insert an ovipositor through softer wood.

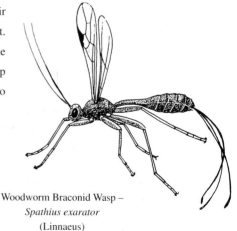

Woodworm Braconid Wasp –
Spathius exarator
(Linnaeus)

Chapter 8: Control of Indoor Insect Pests

What's the use of wasting dynamite when insect-powder will do?

Senator Carter Glass[7]

The information given here should be sufficient to eliminate most problems encountered indoors, but in cases of severe infestations, it may be necessary to contact a reputable pest control firm. The species or groups are arranged alphabetically. It should be remembered that the majority of the Irish insect fauna is completely harmless and that non-pest species should be returned to the wild.

Ants

These insects can be easily controlled by destroying their nests with boiling water or an insecticide. Generally, garden ants will be found nesting within 6m of the infested premises. If the nest cannot be located or is inaccessible, baits containing boric acid or hydramethylnon can be used. These chemicals are carried back to the nest by the workers where they poison the inhabitants. In industrial premises, additional protection will be obtained by painting insecticidal lacquer on the points of entry, pipe runs and skirting boards. Boric acid powder or other insecticides may be also pumped into wall or floor cavities.

The insect development inhibitor methoprene is an effective bait for Pharaoh's ant and has eradicated this pest in hospitals. The chemical was mixed with dried powdered liver, honey, sponge cake and water.

If it is necessary to use an insecticide where food is present, please ensure that it is safe.

7 Unpublished speech to the US Democratic Caucus, 1913

Bed Bugs

Since bed bugs are adept at hiding, a thorough cleaning of floors, walls, beds and bedding is essential. Remember that infestations have even been traced to bed-boards. It is also important to scrape out cracks in floorboards and walls or under the skirting boards. With light infestations, it may be sufficient then to use a normal household insecticide, for example an aerosol containing pyrethroids. Periodic inspections should be made to ensure that all the bed bugs have been killed.

In serious cases, it is advisable to contact the local health board or a pest eradication firm. Spraying with persistent insecticides has proved successful. Nowadays, fumigation of premises is a less popular technique but it may be still necessary for individual items of furniture which are infested.

Beetles

Bacon (Larder) and Hide Beetles

Bacon (larder) and hide beetle infestations can often be traced to neglected food, insanitary conditions or birds' nests. These insects can occur in the rubbish chutes from flats.

In museums, control methods include low or high temperatures, fumigants (including Vapona) and moth-proofing solutions. In industrial premises, including bacon stores, heavy infestations may require the use of a pest eradication firm and can involve fumigation. Preventative measures include the checking of all incoming goods, clean premises, the filling in of all cracks and crevices with concrete, mortar or a suitable alternative, screening of all windows, ventilators and other openings and finally containers with tight-fitting lids. Re-using old sacks in stores can cause infestations and these should be carefully checked.

Contact insecticides are successful in eliminating populations. If insects have been found attacking bacon or ham, the action taken will depend on the extent of the damage. If it is slight, the affected portion can be cut out and then burnt. However, larvae may have burrowed deeply into the meat and destruction may be the only proper course of action.

Biscuit Beetles

Trace the source of the infestation by looking for likely food substances in the rooms where the adults are commonest. Sometimes, rodent baits can be the source of the problem in industrial and other premises. In houses, the species is sometimes introduced in dried flower arrangements. Destroy the larval feeding material if possible and thoroughly clean the area. If the infected object needs to be retained, use a puffer pack of carbaryl insect powder or an aerosol insecticide containing diazinon.

The same treatment applies to tobacco beetles.

Carpet Beetles

In homes, the first sign of an infestation is usually the appearance of beetles on windows. The best method of control is by diligent searching and cleaning. If carpet beetles are involved, take all clothes, bedding and so on out of storage and examine them carefully. If the insects are present, wash or dry-clean all items. In addition, vacuum clean or scrub the inside of the cupboard. Infestations in textiles can be effectively controlled by bagging and freezing garments to –18°C for two weeks.

If the legs of a piece of furniture are uneven, there may be small gaps between them and the floor, and carpet beetles can live in such places, so move the objects to check underneath them. If possible, inspect the undersides of carpets and underlays. Washing has been recommended for killing off the eggs. Other sources of infestation are old birds' nests and neglected packets of food. These should be destroyed.

Death-Watch Beetles

See under **Furniture Beetles**

False Powder-Post Beetles

See under **Furniture Beetles**

Flour Beetles

In houses, destroy all infested food, clean the whole area thoroughly and then use a long-lasting but safe spray insecticide. Infested mills, warehouses and other commercial premises will need professional fumigation to eradicate any serious infestations.

Furniture Beetles (Woodworm)

The following advice also relates to death-watch, powder-post, house longhorn beetles and other wood-boring beetles.

There are now commercial insecticides available which are extremely effective in eradicating infestations of furniture beetles. These are readily available in hardware shops and elsewhere. The chemicals can be purchased in quantities varying from small aerosol sprays to drums. Please follow all the instructions carefully, especially regarding ventilation.

As well as treating the holes, it is essential to brush or spray *all* surfaces of infected furniture (drawers, backing, underneath and even the surfaces of feet). If only the holes are treated, then larvae may survive inside elsewhere in the wood. But do also use the special injectors to spray the insecticide into the holes, and do this first, before you treat the surfaces, so that you can see, by the dampness, which holes have been treated and which not.

In the case of valuable furniture, test a small area with the insecticide in case it might cause damage to the polish or surface. If insecticides are a problem, fumigation is an option.

Special insecticidal polishes are now on the market and if used regularly, they will give protection against attacks. Also remember that even if an object shows no flight holes, it cannot be inferred that there are no woodworm present.

Attacks are less likely if the furniture is kept in a warm, well-ventilated room. Care should be taken not to introduce the species into a house in old timber or second-hand objects, especially ones containing plywood.

If woodworm is found in structural timbers, it may be necessary to employ a professional pest firm to completely eradicate the infestation. A reputable firm will also provide a guarantee which could be useful when selling the property. With minor infestations, the treatment may be a simple matter. In attics, lift up the floorboards and apply the insecticidal fluid to the exposed surfaces of all wood rafters, joists and tie beams. Also treat the floorboards thoroughly before refitting them.

With floors in rooms, lift up the floorboards and replace any seriously affected one with new, pre-treated boards. With salvageable ones, clean all accessible surfaces and apply the insecticide thoroughly before re-laying. Make sure to extend the treatment to joists and frames.

With painted wood, strip off the paint with a commercial stripper before applying the insecticide. In some instances, it may be necessary to remove joinery timber (skirting boards, picture rails, panelling) in order to treat the side next to the wall. Incidentally, if you are building your own house, it is very cost-effective to have all the timbers treated during construction.

Ground Beetles

Since the beetles normally enter houses by crawling under doors, draught-excluding strips can be used to exclude them.

Hide Beetles

See under **Bacon Beetles**

House Longhorn Beetles

See under **Furniture Beetles**

Larder Beetles

See under **Bacon Beetles**

Lesser Mealworm Beetles

Prevention of infestations is the first line of defence with this species. All food brought into piggeries or poultry houses should be carefully inspected before use. Once an infestation becomes established, it is only possible to control it when the broiler house or piggery is empty and the litter has been removed. Very thorough cleaning is essential. Dig over any areas containing the larvae, and then spray with an insecticide. Pay particular attention to and spray all crevices which could harbour the species.

Mealworm Beetles

Search for the source of the infestation and destroy any infected food. Puff a household (crawling insect) insecticide into any nearby crevices after they have been cleaned out.

Mould Beetles

The beetles can be easily killed using ordinary powder or aerosol insecticides. However, to prevent reinfestation, it is necessary to remove the damp conditions which they require. Rooms should be kept warm and well aired. If infestations continue to recur, the premises probably has a problem with condensation, which will need to be rectified. Serious infestations in granaries, warehouses, and similar buildings may require professional fumigation.

Pea and Bean Beetles

See **Seed Beetles**

Powder-Post Beetles

The most practical way of preventing attacks is to season all wood with the bark still intact, but it is necessary to guard against rot from too damp conditions. For other advice, see under **Furniture Beetles**.

Saw-Toothed Grain Beetles

See the advice given under **Weevils—Grain Weevils**. In addition, cooling is another practical method of eliminating this pest. Air is drawn from outside through the grain to reduce the temperature to below 18.3°C. The beetles cannot breed under such conditions.

It should be noted that infestation does not take place in the field, but only after grain has been put into store or into infested bags. Only a few insects are necessary to initiate a serious infestation.

Seed Beetles (Pea and Bean Beetles)

In homes, packets infested by pea and bean beetles should be destroyed. In warehouses, fumigation can be carried out with methyl bromide, aluminium phosphide, or a choice between ethylene dichloride and carbon tetrachloride. The choice of fumigant will depend on storage conditions and the treatment should be undertaken only by a qualified pest firm.

Spider Beetles

These beetles thrive best where food residues are allowed to accumulate, where rodents are numerous or in birds' nests. Trace the source of the infestation and remove any items which are being eaten. If possible, infected objects should be destroyed. Cleanliness and prevention are better than control measures for these insects because they are not very susceptible to insecticides.

Tobacco Beetle

See under **Biscuit Beetle**

Bluebottles

See under **Flies—Blowflies**

Booklice

Insecticide treatments or fumigation normally give only temporary relief from booklice infestations. If conditions are suitable, the insects will merely recolonise from natural sources. However, a thorough airing and drying of an infested area along with the removal of all signs of mould is usually successful. If a premises is kept dry so that the minute moulds which are the food supply cannot survive, then the insects should disappear. If such heating is not successful, then the premises should be inspected for any structural faults which may cause dampness. Because of the Irish climate, dampness is a problem in many houses. Gas fires should not be used for drying out a premises, as they produce moisture.

Cheese-Skipper

The deep burrowing activities of the maggots means that affected food should be destroyed. Problems with this species can be avoided if foods likely to be attacked are stored below 9°C, because the cheese-skipper cannot breed below this temperature. If they become established in a building they are very difficult to eradicate.

Cockroaches

The current tendency is to reduce the area treated and the quantity of insecticide applied by using the crack-and-crevice technique. Small amounts are introduced into cracks and crevices where the insects hide or through which they may gain access inside. The insecticide may be applied in liquid or dust form or in a bait. Dusts tend to be more successful, as cockroaches crawling over them are more likely to pick up a lethal dose. Toxic baits can be in paste or pellet form. Boric acid powder has been used with considerable success in some instances.

Since many infestations occur where food is being prepared, it is important to choose safe insecticides and to use them with great care. Food preparation surfaces should be covered and cooking utensils removed. In some hospitals and the food industry, dry-ice fumigation has worked. In tests at 26°C, a minimum concentration (21%) of carbon dioxide over a twenty-four hour period killed all German cockroaches and their egg cases. This type of fumigation has the advantage of being safe but is impractical for building disinfestation.

Sticky and electrified traps may help to reduce populations. Several treatments may be necessary to eliminate the cockroaches and commercial premises are advised that the best protection may be provided by a specialist making regular inspections.

Earwigs

Since these creatures are nocturnal, tightly closed windows will usually prevent them from crawling indoors. Sometimes, earwigs enter premises by climbing up overflow outlets from wash-basins or baths, particularly if vegetation is growing near the outlet. This problem can be solved by fitting a fine mesh over the outlet which will still allow the water to pass through.

Fleas

Flea infestations cannot survive in premises which are regularly swept and cleaned thoroughly, as the larvae are eliminated. If there are persistent problems, it is necessary to identify what species is involved.

Human fleas normally infest bedrooms. If you are bitten in bed, you can trap the flea by turning back the bedclothes and quickly dabbing a moist bar of soap on the offending specimen. To get rid of the infestation, the floor can be first dusted with a safe insecticide. Then thoroughly clean carpets, rugs and bedding. Remove any fluff or dirt from between the floorboards.

Cat fleas and dog fleas usually originate from pet animals, so carefully clean the sleeping area and also apply a suitable insecticide to the fur. It is often advisable to burn the pet's bedding and sweep the area. Insecticides which could be poisonous to the pet should not be used, as cats, for instance, could lick them off their coats.

If you have to visit flea-infested premises, you should apply a repellent such as dimethylphthalate to your clothing.

Flies

Blowflies (Bluebottles)

In domestic premises, it is usually sufficient to keep food in refrigerators or covered when left in the open. Dustbins should be kept clean to stop infestations originating from them. This precaution also applies to hotels, cafés and other food establishments. In addition, owners of such premises must keep yards and drains clean.

In bacon-factories, blowflies can be a problem. Some protection can be obtained from soaking the bacon in brine or wrapping it in hessian. In addition, non-poisonous insecticides have been successfully applied in pea-flour to bacon-sides.

In fish-shops, plastic containers and glass-topped refrigerated showcases will both provide protection and also reduce fly-attracting odours. Insect electrocutors will help to kill any blowflies coming indoors. Cleanliness of the premises, fish boxes and so forth is essential.

Cluster Flies

Unfortunately, it is almost impossible to prevent annual invasions once these insects have selected a particular house. When they have accumulated, the flies can be killed using an insecticidal spray and the dead ones sucked up in a vacuum cleaner. Alternatively, the live insects may be sucked up into the vacuum cleaner's bag into which insecticide has already been added. Allow several hours to elapse before emptying the bag and do it in the open air.

Drone Flies

Infestations can easily be eliminated by tracing where the rat-tailed maggots are living (polluted drains and ditches, for example) and cleaning up the larval habitat.

House Flies

Indoors, the adults can be controlled by the use of aerosol insecticides, which are widely available in shops. For those who do not like to use chemicals or where there are pet fish tanks, fly 'swatters' are highly effective. Sticky fly papers are unsightly, but they are effective.

Dustbins should be kept clean and tidy with tight-fitting lids. It is useful to spray them inside with an insecticide. Refuse bags must be removed regularly and be stored in such a way that they cannot be holed or otherwise damaged thus allowing access to adults.

Fly screens and electrocutors (often fitted with an ultra-violet light) are helpful in hospitals, shops, food-factories, restaurants and other premises serving food. It is interesting that a curtain of air moving across a doorway can be effective in reducing the numbers of adults entering indoors. An air curtain is created by a powerful fan blowing air across a doorway.

Kitchen Flies

This pest may be controlled by tracing the breeding site and removing all the larval food material. It is essential for public houses, etc. serving food to ensure that decaying vegetable material is not allowed to accumulate in or around bins placed inside the premises or under the bar.

Moth Flies

Aerosol fly sprays will kill the adults. The immature stages can be eliminated by cleaning out the breeding sites, especially any slimy areas around sinks, overflow traps, drains and shores.

Stable Flies

In houses, it is usually sufficient to spray any specimens which come indoors. However if there is a persistent problem with the species, remove any straw or rotting vegetation near the premises. If they are present in garden compost, spread it out thinly on the ground.

Urinal Flies

Normal hygiene and cleanliness will eliminate infestations of the urinal fly.

Vinegar Flies

Outbreaks should be dealt with by destroying the material in which they are breeding.

Lesser Grain Borer

See under **Weevils — Grain Weevils**

Lice

The practice of 'popping' lice with the fingernails can be dangerous and should not be used—typhus can be spread in this manner.

Crab (Pubic) Lice

These may be eliminated by using a modern insecticide. It is important to repeat the treatment a week later to kill off any newly-hatched lice. Treatment may include shaving of the pubic hair.

Body Lice

With general lousiness, it is important to reduce the infestation as quickly as possible. Without their human host, lice quickly starve or die from cold, though taking clothes off at night is not enough. Washing clothes in hot water and particularly ironing the seams will kill both eggs and lice. Alternatively, clothing may be either fumigated or heat treated (over 70°C for an hour). In addition, body hair should be shaved off and the person bathed.

Insecticides can be applied to all articles of clothing in mass epidemics.

Head Lice

Head lice are not caused by poor hygiene. They are simply passed from head to head, especially among children.

Children's hair should be checked regularly, looking carefully behind the ears, at the back of the head, on the neck, crown and under fringes. Scratching the scalp is usually the first sign that a child has head lice, but by this time they have probably been in the hair for several weeks. Lice may be detected by examining the scalp or using a special comb available in chemists.

If one of the family is infected, ask your public health nurse, local health clinic, doctor or chemist for a suitable treatment. Follow their advice and instructions carefully. Head lice have become resistant to some previously effective insecticides but modern clinical preparations should soon clear up the problem.

Check that no-one else is affected, not just in the family but other possible contacts too, such as your children's friends. To avoid re-infestation, disinfect clothes and personal items such as combs, brushes and hats after initial treatment. Check every time the hair is washed. Parents should impress on children the importance of not using other people's combs or borrowing items of clothing such as hats, ribbons and scarves.

Mealy Bugs

Because of their life-style and wax coverings, it is sometimes difficult to eradicate these insects. In houses, mealybugs can be removed from plants using a small brush dipped in alcohol. In greenhouses, it may be necessary to use systemic insecticides. An Australian species of ladybird has been used in some British greenhouses with relatively high temperatures.

Midges, Biting

Because of the nature of the larval habitats, it is virtually impossible to eradicate these pests. In areas where these insects are a serious problem, protection will be provided indoors by installing fly screens. Highly allergic people should stay indoors and keep windows and doors closed. The regular use of an aerosol insecticide should be of some help. In addition, insect repellents can be applied to exposed skin.

Advice on treating the symptoms of the highly irritating bite are described in chapter 9.

Mosquitoes

Adults can be killed indoors with aerosol insecticides. Fly screens can be fitted to the premises of allergic people.

Larval mosquitoes in their aquatic habitats may be controlled by the use of the microbial insecticide *Bacillus thuringiensis* var. *israelensis*, a method which has the advantage of not harming other wildlife. Sometimes, mosquitoes will breed in bird baths or stagnant water in discarded or neglected containers. These should be emptied regularly if there is a serious problem with biting mosquitoes.

The treatment of bites is discussed in chapter 9.

Moths

House and Clothes Moths

The first line of defence is vigilance. Regular household cleaning will often discourage attacks. Food should not be left neglected in larders. Areas of carpet inaccessible to vacuum-cleaners should be periodically inspected.

Commercial moth-proofing agents may be purchased in hardware shops and other stores, either in aerosols or in other forms. However, they have their limitations, so please follow the instructions carefully. Commercial moth-proofing of carpets and furnishings is not always completely successful, and there are incidents in Ireland of such items being badly damaged by moths. It is important, therefore, not to be overconfident about such treatments. Instead, remain vigilant and if you detect any trouble, use a moth-proofer in the affected area before any serious infestation develops.

A good early-warning system is to look out for adults indoors and, if they are seen in numbers, to trace where they are coming from. Initially, they will usually be confined to the room in which they emerged. Sometimes, populations can live inside upholstered furniture and may remain unobserved for a long period.

It is very effective to dry-clean or wash garments to be stored, before putting them away in sealed plastic bags or in plastic or paper wrapping. Such barriers will prevent female moths from gaining access. Moth balls (naphthalene) may be inserted in the bags as a further deterrent. Moth-repellents can also be hung in wardrobes or cupboards. Cold storage (c. 5°C) can be effective. Stored clothing should be checked frequently. Do not store woollen articles in attics during the summer.

If an infestation does occur in a premises, badly damaged articles should be destroyed. Sometimes, infestations may be traced to old birds' nests, and these should be removed. Items of clothing which can be salvaged should be thoroughly brushed and shaken to remove eggs and caterpillars. Infestations in textiles can be effectively controlled by bagging and freezing garments to −18°C for two weeks.

Pyralid Moths

In households, it is sufficient to destroy infected goods. In shops, care must be taken where food could be contaminated by an insecticide. Efficient stock rotation and inspection are the best deterrents. Nowadays, insect-repellent coatings containing pyrethrum are sometimes used by manufacturers on cartons and wrapping paper. In warehouses, infestations of pyralid moths and other pest insects are more difficult to control, since the pests have the potential to adjust quickly to prevailing conditions. All grain-handling equipment should be thoroughly cleaned before harvest. Cleanliness is of great importance because accumulations which are frequently overlooked (such as empty feed sacks, dust, grain-based rodenticides) can be serious sources of infestations.

There are three main chemical methods of treatment:

- Fumigation, which uses insecticides in gaseous forms and requires sealed conditions

- Space treatment, using spray (droplet) insecticides, which, when dispersed in the air, make direct contact with the targeted insects – pyrethrum is found to be useful, as it irritates insects that have settled on walls and ceilings, causing them to fly through the mist where they pick up a lethal dose of the insecticide.

- Residual insecticides which are applied in liquid or solid form—these will kill moths as soon as they emerge and prevent them from laying eggs

Protective insecticides can be applied in bins, in joints, seams and crevices, on walls, floors and ledges. In the food industry, it is essential that only approved insecticides are used. Success in treating bulk grain will depend on proper mixing, a fresh spray mixture, where it is applied, the pressure of application and the moisture/temperature of the grain.

Non-chemical methods of control include temperature (either high or low depending on the stored goods), physical barriers (such as protective packaging), ionising radiation and non-ionising radiation (such as infra-red heaters, electric fields, visible and ultra-violet light). In many cases, physical methods can be combined with the judicious use of chemicals to enhance the effectiveness of both. In the food-handling industry, cleanliness is an essential requirement for helping to prevent infestations of pest insects.

Scale Insects

Some indoor plants may be treated by wiping the scales off leaves and stems using a soft rag, sponge or small paint brush dipped in soapy water. Insecticides such as pyrethrum are effective when used on the crawlers before they have settled.

Seaweed Flies

Indoors, this insect can be easily controlled by using an aerosol insecticide when invasions occur.

Silverfish and Firebrats

Many Irish people are happy to have silverfish living in their houses. However, it does sometimes become necessary to eradicate both silverfish and firebrats in food factories, bakeries and museums where there may be valuable papers, textiles and so on. It is not easy to kill them with insecticides, but it is often possible to eliminate them by creating unfavourable conditions. Damp rooms, for example, should be thoroughly heated and aired. If the air is kept warm and dry, silverfish will not survive for long. If insecticides must be used, a puffer pack of carbaryl insect powder is often recommended.

Springtails

Since springtails are characteristic of humid and moist conditions, it is usually sufficient to dry and thoroughly air any affected areas. In addition, remove any decomposing or decaying vegetable material, including wood.

Wasps, Social

In houses, aerosol or spray insecticides are very successful in killing individual wasps which have strayed indoors.

Some types of windows used in Ireland actually force foraging workers to come indoors. These have sections which slope outwards from the top when open. Wasps hunting on the window pane upon encountering such an overhead obstruction will simply fly indoors through the open window rather than go around it. A simple fly screen fitted to such windows, or any window where wasps enter the house, will eliminate the problem.

Trapping in a jam jar is also effective in or around the home. Place a small amount of jam in the bottom of the jar and then fill about a quarter full with water. Add a few drops of beer if available and two or three drops of washing-up liquid. Place a hand over the top and shake the jar. Smear a tiny amount of the jam inside the jar. Cover the top with a piece of paper, fix with a rubber band and pierce the top with a pencil. The hole must be small or the wasps can escape. The wasps enter the trap and eventually slip into the water where they drown. The traps can be placed around dustbins, on window sills, on walls or any place where they will attract the wasps away from where they might cause problems.

The eradication of nests is complex and can be dangerous to inexperienced people. Small nests in situations such as compost heaps may be tackled by the householder, however. It is essential to treat all nests at dusk or after dark when the wasps are inactive and to leave the area as quickly as possible. Wear gloves and, if possible, cover the face with netting (such as a bee keeper's veil) to prevent stings. Tuck trousers into socks and wear wellington boots. Make sure that these are closed at the top, as otherwise wasps can crawl inside. The looser the clothing the better, since wasps can sting through most ordinary fabrics and so it helps to leave space between the body and the outer clothing.

Use a puffer pack containing derris dust, carbaryl or a proprietary wasp nest killer to eliminate the nest. The powder is puffed into the entrance and left for 24 hours. Wasps passing through will carry the dust inside into the nest. If activity continues, repeat the treatment.

Large nests are best left to professional eradicators. This also applies to most nests in attics and under eaves. In the confines of a roof space, if anything goes wrong, there is normally only one quick way out —through the ceiling, which is usually painful and may require expensive repairs. With nests under the eaves, angry wasps may cascade out of the hole when the insecticide touches them. If the wasps fall on the person and he or she is on a ladder, panic may result in a fall or serious accident.

There is one exception—a very small nest which is fully exposed in a roof space can be tackled. Take a long kitchen knife and a large polythene bag. Open the bag, place it over the nest and then slip the knife inside to cut the nest down. Pour water into the bag containing the nest. Fill and tie it. This type of method was recommended as long ago as 1770 and is still cheap, easy and effective.

Food-serving premises including shops can reduce infestations of workers by using electrocutors, but it is essential to clean out the collecting pans regularly. If slow-acting insecticides are placed in baits, the workers will carry the poisoned food back to the nest and poison the inhabitants.

Wasps can cause major problems in industrial premises. If large numbers are entering indoors, electrocutors may not kill them all, resulting in angry individuals crawling out of the collecting trays and stinging people. It may be necessary to use other methods to discourage wasps from entering. All windows can be covered with a fine nylon mesh and 'air curtains' are useful at doors. Such a curtain is created by a powerful fan blowing air across a doorway. Plastic strip curtains are also successful. Baiting has proved to be inefficient when used alone on commercial premises but may be of some use in an integrated wasp control programme.

The treatment of stings is discussed in chapter 9.

Weevils

Grain Weevils

To prevent infestations, good storage and hygienic conditions in a damp-proof building are essential. It is necessary to make regular inspections and to have a good cleaning regime. Debris should not be allowed to accumulate. Grain should be kept at as low a temperature as possible. Rotation is recommended to prevent the accumulation of old stocks.

If an infestation occurs, non-toxic insecticides or fumigation can be used to eliminate the insects. When restocking after an infestation, spray or dust the walls and floors with the insecticides. If the grain is sweet and the infestation has not been serious, it can still be fed to livestock without treatment.

Vine Weevil

Indoor pot plants may be protected by drenching the soil with insecticides such as pyrethroids or by adding naphthalene (mothball) flakes to the compost when potting up. In glasshouses, the species can be eliminated by good hygiene, regular inspections and insecticides. Spraying with pyrethroids is effective. Dust pyrethroids can be added to the compost.

For those who do not like to use chemicals, it is possible to take a plant from its pot and shake it over a newspaper. Any vine weevils (adults, larvae or pupae) can then be easily detected and killed by dropping them into boiling water before the plant is repotted in sterile soil or compost. Nematodes have recently become commercially available as a means of biological control.

Wood-Boring Weevils

Treatment is similar to that recommended under **Furniture Beetles**. However, since these insects are closely associated with wood attacked by wet rot fungus, it is also necessary to treat this problem or to remove all the affected timber.

Wharf Borer

Control measures are similar to those for furniture beetles but the damp wood must be dried out or, preferably, cut away and replaced.

Whiteflies

The parasitic wasp *Encarsia formosa* Gahan has been very successfully used to control whitefly infestations at temperatures above 21°C. It can be easily introduced on cards or leaves containing parasitised scales. Supplies may be purchased from commercial dealers. In houses, a spraying of pyrethrum should suffice if applied to both sides of the leaves at frequent intervals. In greenhouses, the same chemical or other contact or systematic insecticides (such as permethrin, bioresmethrin, dimethoate) may be used at weekly intervals. Some whitefly populations are now resistant to certain commercial insecticides so if one is unsuccessful, it may be necessary to try another. In the case of edible crops, the manufacturer's instructions must be carefully followed.

Woodworm

See **Furniture Beetle**

Chapter 9: Insects and Human Health

*'For many died from carbuncles, and boils, and
botches which grew on the legs and under the
arms; others from passion of the head, as if thrown
into a frenzy; others by vomiting blood.'*[8]

Many insects are completely harmless. Some can do damage to goods or property, but are not directly harmful to humans. Others, however, can bite or sting, and in some cases, the bites can be very irritating and the stings extremely painful. In a few cases, the bites or stings are also dangerous, either because the affected person has an allergic reaction, or because this is one of the ways in which insects can carry disease. Insects that don't bite or sting can also carry disease, by contaminating food or items that people use.

Insect Bites and Stings

Ant Stings

Stinging ants, including the Pharaoh's ant, Roger's ant and the Argentine ant, can occur in buildings. The stings of ants in this country are generally less severe than those of bees or wasps because they contain less venom. However, Pharaoh's ant can rupture the delicate skin of infants in hospitals harbouring this pest. The common black ant, although it does not sting, can squirt formic acid, which may cause mild skin irritation.

Bee Stings

The venom of the bee is very complex and contains histamine. Unlike the wasp's, the sting of the bee is barbed. As a result, each bee can only sting once, for when the offending insect is brushed

8. Contemporary account of Bubonic Plague by Friar John Clyn of Kilkenny city, describing the disease which affected Ireland in 1349. The Annals of Ireland (ed. R. Butler), 1849.

141

away, the stinging apparatus, along with the poison sac, may be left in the wound. The sac will continue to pump venom so do not seize it. This will simply force more venom into the wound. Instead, scrape the sting out with your fingernail or a knife.

Then wash the area well with soap and water. Ice packs will relieve the pain and reduce swelling, and an anti-histamine preparation can be sprayed on, spread as a cream or taken as tablets or capsules.

Patients with a moderate or severe reaction should rest for several hours. It is essential to get anyone stung in the mouth to a doctor or a hospital as a matter of urgency. Otherwise, swelling may make breathing and eating difficult or impossible. In severe or allergic reactions, victims must be treated by a medical practitioner with great speed. Epinephrine (adrenaline) injections have been recommended by Frazier and Brown (1980) to abort anaphylactic shock. People with known hypersensitivity should carry an emergency kit and some form of notification of their condition.

Wasp Stings

When a wasp uses its sting, it injects into its foe a small quantity of venom produced by special glands. Each wasp can deliver more than one sting, and the effect multiplies. The venom is a complex mixture of compounds including histamine and has a pH which is very near neutral.

The sting affects different people in different ways, depending on the physical condition and age of the victim. For most, it causes a small swelling, a little pain and some irritation of the skin. The effects may last from a few minutes to several hours before subsiding. Other people are more adversely affected. The swelling may last days. It may be more painful and there may be other symptoms such as chest constriction, difficult breathing, nausea or dizziness.

A sting may prove fatal for a small minority. The earliest record is that of the first Pharaoh of Egypt, who is reputed to have been killed by a sting about 3000 B.C. In England and Wales, seventy deaths were caused by wasps between 1949 and 1969. Death usually results from respiratory obstruction or anaphylactic shock. Victims can die within an hour.

Unfortunately, we do not know of a satisfactory cure for wasp stings. Non-allergic people can wash the site with soap and water, followed by the application of an anti-histamine preparation. The anti-histamine can be sprayed on, spread as a cream or taken as tablets or capsules. The sprays normally also contain a mild narcotic to reduce pain. Any form of cooling (an ice pack, for example) also helps.

Patients with a moderate or severe reaction should rest for several hours. It is essential to get anyone stung in the mouth to a doctor or a hospital as a matter of urgency. Otherwise, swelling may make breathing and eating difficult or impossible. In severe or allergic reactions, victims must be treated by a medical practitioner with great speed. People with known hypersensitivity should carry an emergency kit and some form of notification of their condition.

Flea Bites

Fleas are a nuisance to most of us, but some people are sensitive to the secretions that they inject into their bites. These secretions have a sensitising effect, which means that although the initial bites may have no effect, subsequent ones can flare up. They become hard, red and itchy. People may eventually gain an immunity.

In general, the worst a flea-bite can do is become infected. Since it can itch intensely, this is a possibility especially among children. The bites should be washed with soap and water. Also apply an antiseptic and treat the bite, if necessary, with anti-itching medications and lotions, including calamine lotion and oral anti-histamines. If signs of infection develop, consult your medical practitioner.

Midge Bites

'One midge is an entomological curiosity, a thousand can be hell' (D. S. Kettle). These insects can occur in such numbers that they affect tourism or forestry. Landing rates of a thousand per hour have been recorded, but for most humans, five bites per hour is considered an acceptable limit. Sensitivity to the bites is thought to be responsible for an allergic response in horses in Britain known as 'sweet itch'.

The female is the attacker, possessing mouth-parts like miniature scissors and a stabbing proboscis. She plunges this into her victim, after cutting a small incision in the skin. Often the victim is unaware of the insect's presence until bitten—resulting in consternation. The bite is painful, raises welts and itches like mad. The irritation can last for weeks.

Scratching can cause secondary infections, but the midges themselves are not known to transmit any human diseases. Some extremely allergic people have had to be treated with adrenaline and anti-histamines. Personal protection can be obtained by wearing relatively wide mesh veils impregnated with repellent. Alternatively, repellent creams or lotions can be rubbed on exposed parts of the body.

Mosquito Bites

To most people, mosquito bites are simply an irritation. When the female bites, her saliva, which acts as an anti-coagulant and diluent, causes a reaction. There may be an immediate reaction with a delayed spot or blister.

There is a great deal of individual variation in reactions to mosquito bites. Irritation can be alleviated by applying calamine or anti-histamine cream to the spot. Alternatively, anti-histamine can be taken orally. Scratching should be avoided.

Mosquitoes can cause severe problems in parts of Ireland. In a seaside area of north County Dublin, for example, the bites of *Culiseta annulata* have produced allergic reactions in a small number of people. One woman had such a serious reaction that she was forced to stay indoors for long periods. Recently, an infestation in a hospital resulted in lumps appearing on patients in a ward.

Repellent chemicals can be used for personal protection where mosquitoes are known to be a problem.

Diseases Caused by Insects

In Ireland, there are now relatively few serious insect-borne diseases, and this decline is due to great improvements in hygiene. However, insects have been responsible for large numbers of deaths in historical times and these could reappear with devastating effects on our society.

Louse-Borne Relapsing Fever

This disease is spread among humans when infected lice are crushed or ruptured, usually between the fingernails. The causative spirochaete *Borrelia recurrentis* is then released and enters the body through scratches or sores and cuts. Strangely, it is not transmitted by louse bites. The disease is characterised by high temperatures and a violent fever. There are generalised aches and pains with nose-bleeding followed by profuse sweating. Relapses are common. Mortality can be as high as 30 per cent.

Louse-borne relapsing fever was common in Ireland from 1800 to 1850. There was a severe outbreak between the end of 1817 and the end of March 1819. Over 100,000 people were treated in fever hospitals and dispensaries throughout the island and some 4225 died. Prior to the epidemic, weather conditions were bad and turf, which was the main source of fuel and heat, could not be dried. In addition, the potatoes were wet and the oatmeal bad.

Malaria

Malaria is commonly associated with the tropics, but a form of this disease has been transmitted by mosquitoes in Ireland. Malaria begins with a chill, accompanied by shivering and other symptoms. This is quickly followed by fever, which ends with profuse sweating. Similar attacks follow one another at variable intervals, depending on the type of malaria.

Caused by the single-celled animal or protozoan *Plasmodium vivax*, which ruptures the red cells of the blood, it is spread by mosquitoes of the genus *Anopheles*, four of which occur on this island. The form known from here (benign tertian malaria), however, is less serious than the widespread tropical malaria (malignant tertian malaria) caused by *Plasmodium falciparum*.

The term 'ague' was used until the late nineteenth century as an all-encompassing term for various fevers including malaria. As a result, it is very difficult to ascertain the nature of particular 'ague' epidemics mentioned in Irish historical records. Indeed, most are likely to have been caused by typhus or influenza rather than malaria, and the 'Irish ague' that paralysed Cromwell's army in Ireland in 1649 was probably typhus. There was little malaria in Ireland at that time according to Boate, Cromwell's 'Doctor of Physik to the State of Ireland', writing in 1652. Some deaths from 'ague' were reported from Ireland in 1878–81 and Graves (quoted by Davidson 1892) says 'formerly ague was rather of common occurrence in some marshy districts near Dublin'.

An exception is the incidence of malaria in Cork described by Cummins (1957). The author quotes a doctor, stating 'Before the year 1844, malaria was almost unknown in Cork and then it commenced, year after year, increasing its ravages, until it became a perfect plague in 1857. In my registry alone, in that year (the Ballintemple–Blackrock Dispensary), 175 cases occurred.' For the years 1854–60, 663 cases were reported from the Ballincollig district of Cork. The Cork Medical Society recorded 917 cases. The Crimean War (1853–6) may have been a contributory factor in causing the epidemic due to the large numbers of infective soldiers, belonging to regiments normally stationed in Ireland, returning home from war service. In addition, it was a period of warm summers and drainage work may also have provided ideal mosquito breeding sites.

The importation of malaria from other parts of the world is a matter of some concern. It may seem unlikely that the disease could re-establish itself in Ireland because it might be necessary for large numbers of native mosquitoes to contract the disease from infected malaria patients and spread it to other people. However, in 1983 two cases of tropical malaria were contracted in Britain by people living close to Gatwick Airport, who had not travelled to any malarious country. Transmission was attributed to infective tropical *Anopheles* escaping from intercontinental aircraft. Besides these cases there have been twenty-one cases of 'airport malaria' reported in association with other European airports.

Foreign mosquitoes are known to have arrived in Ireland by aircraft in the past. Increasing air travel, more rapid turnaround times, and more regular services to exotic locations make it likely that some Irish people could contract malaria or some other mosquito-borne disease in Ireland. Each year, cases of people who contracted the disease abroad are reported. Between 1982 and 1993, the number has varied between nine and forty-one in the Republic. Global warming may also favour a return of malaria.

Pediculosis

This is a form of skin disease or dermatitis resulting from the irritation caused by multiple louse bites. When the bites are scratched, secondary infections can occur. These include impetigo, furunculosis and eczema.

Plague

The connection between fleas and plague was not made until the 1890s. The main sources are the black rat and the plague flea (*Xenopsylla*). *Yersinia pestis*, the plague bacillus, is chiefly a parasite of rats, and human infections are only an accidental consequence of an outbreak amongst rodents.

Nevertheless, the consequences can be devastating. A bite from a rat flea may result in the injection of 25,000–100,000 bacilli beneath the skin—frequently an inoculation which overwhelms the human immune system. The bacilli multiply in the nearest lymph glands. These are normally in the groin or armpits. After two to five days, a painful lump develops (the bubo). This is usually livid red or purplish. It may swell to the size of an orange, resulting in intense pain before it breaks or suppurates. The mortality rate without treatment can reach 80 per cent, with death occurring within five days. This form of the disease is known as bubonic plague.

There are also septicaemic and pneumonic plagues associated with it. The first is an infection mainly of the bloodstream and can kill within hours. The second is caught through contagion, like influenza, and has a very high fatality rate. In the nursery rhyme 'Ring a ring o' roses, A pocket full of posies, Ah-tishoo! Ah-tishoo! We all fall down,' the first line refers to the rash and the second to flowers to take away the smell. The remainder describes the effects of pneumonic plague.

Plague has probably brought more human grief and fear than any other single disease. A terrible and widespread epidemic occurred about the time of the Emperor Justinian in the sixth century A.D. The original source may have been Central Asia, from which the disease slowly followed the caravan routes. It reached Ireland in A.D. 664, and two-thirds of the population died in the next twenty years. The victims included the joint high kings of Ireland.

The next epidemic in the thirteenth century (the Black Death) killed a quarter of the population of Europe. It reached the east coast of Ireland about early 1348. It seems to have struck Drogheda first and spread rapidly inland. The rat-infested centres of population were hardest hit. Within a few weeks both Dublin and Drogheda were almost completely destroyed. In Dublin, almost 14,000 people died before Christmas. People naturally panicked, fleeing into the countryside or to famous shrines. Thousands (including prelates and nobles) waded into the River Barrow at St Mullins. So terrific were the losses that people commonly thought that the end of the world was near and that all would die. The Anglo-Irish communities suffered most because they lived in the rat-infested towns.

The loss of a huge proportion of the population had devastating effects. Manors were abandoned and boroughs wiped out. Due to scarcity of labour, wages and costs spiralled. Lydon (1973) notes that in the church, the results were disastrous. Due to the deaths within the clergy, many unsuitable people were recruited into the priesthood and religious orders.

Other epidemics, including the Great Plague of London in 1665, flared and smouldered in Europe and these also affected Ireland. Gradually, the disease died out in the eighteenth century. Although plague has now been absent from Ireland for some considerable time, we must guard against the idea that it is a disease of the past. It remains elsewhere in the world, only waiting for the opportunity to take advantage of a weakness in hygiene to strike again.

Typhus

Louse-borne typhus is caused by *Rickettsia prowazeki*, a microscopic organism related to bacteria. It is transmitted to humans by head and body lice in their excrement. It is very seldom passed by a bite. Although the louse dies within twelve days of infection, the infective organism can remain virulent for as long as sixty-six days in the dried excrement. Humans are infected by the organism getting into the bloodstream through scratches (caused by the irritation of the louse bites), or through the lungs, the conjuctiva of the eye or the mucous membrane. The human mortality rate can range from 30 to 60 per cent.

The symptoms at first resemble and are often mistaken for those of influenza. The temperature rises quickly to about 39.5°C. There is a severe headache, chills, pains in the limbs and depression. The rash only appears on the fourth or fifth day on the shoulders and trunk—as pink spots. These later become a deep brownish red, spreading outwards to the hand and feet. They rarely occur on the face. Delirium and extreme weakness follow.

When typhus arrived in Ireland is uncertain, but it may have been the disease that paralysed Cromwell's army in 1649. The first precisely recorded epidemic was that observed in 1708 and the disease was endemic here since the beginning of the eighteenth century. Certainly lice were a terrible problem in the country. Thomas Mouffet (father of 'little Miss Muffet') remarked in his *Theatrum Insectorum* of 1634:

> All Ireland is noted for this, that it swarms almost with lice. But that this proceeds from the beastliness of the people and want of cleanly women to wash them, is manifest, because the English that are more careful to dress themselves, changing and washing their shirts often, have escaped the plague. Hence it is that armies and prisons are so full of lice, the sweat being corrupted by wearing always the same clothes, and from this arises matter for their origin, by the mediation of heat.

There was a large outbreak associated with the potato famine of 1740. During the great Irish epidemic of 1816–19, there were 700,000 cases recorded among six million inhabitants. It continued to be common until 1850, and 1937 was the first year when there were no deaths from typhus in Ireland. In the Republic, one case was reported between 1982 and 1993. This disease was also responsible for the dreaded prison or gaol fever.

Illnesses Spread by Insects

Several illnesses are spread from one person to another by insect carriers. Various flies and other insects which feed on or visit excrement or other waste products may land on a person, on food, drink or crockery, resulting in contamination by disease-causing bacteria. These may be present on the insect's body (especially on the feet and mouth). However the fly's vomit-drops and its faeces are probably more important means of transmission.

Cholera

Cholera is an acute infectious disease of the small intestine caused by the bacterium *Vibrio cholerae*. It is characterised by diarrhoea with severe depletion of body fluids and salts. The most usual means of contracting cholera is through drinking contaminated water, but contaminated food or other drinks can be responsible. Flies may spread the disease by visiting excrement or other sources of contamination and then carrying the bacteria to uninfected food or drink.

The first recorded outbreak of cholera in Ireland occurred throughout the island in 1832. It was in Dublin in March and by May had reached Limerick. There was a widespread European epidemic in 1833 and in Dublin alone there were 5600 deaths. In 1866, there was another outbreak in the same city and the mortality rate in hospitals varied between 42 and 54 per cent. In the midst of this epidemic, which took the lives of nearly 1200 citizens, steps were taken to bring the city into line with sanitary improvements elsewhere and by the end of the century, notable improvements had already been made. There were no cases reported in the Republic between 1982 and 1993.

Food Poisoning

There are numerous species and strains of *Salmonella* which occur in a wide range of different animals and can be transmitted from them to humans. These can be responsible for various degrees of food poisoning. The bacteria can be spread by various means, including some insects, from infected food, drink, dish cloths, work-top surfaces and so on to uncontaminated items. In the Republic, the number of reported cases between 1982 and 1993 varied from 142 to 484 each year.

Shigella dysenteriae which causes dysentery and diarrhoea has been isolated from German cockroaches from the environs of patients in Northern Ireland.

Typhoid Fever

The bacterium responsible is *Salmonella typhi* and it is present in the excrement and urine of infected persons. It can be spread from such waste products in several ways, including by visiting insects. These carry bacteria on their bodies and contaminate food and drink by landing or feeding. Anybody consuming or handling such items can then become infected.

The fever begins with headache, raised temperature and a general feeling of being unwell. Later a rash appears in the form of rose-red spots on the front of the chest and abdomen and on the back. In the second week, there is great weakness, sometimes diarrhoea, flatulence and mental dullness, accompanied by dry and cracked lips and tongues.

In 1899, Dublin had the unenviable reputation of being the unhealthiest city in the United Kingdom and compared very unfavourably in the number of cases of typhoid fever attacking adults over 25. Deaths from this cause were halved after 1903, an improvement mainly attributable to the abolition of the old ashpit privy system, the closing of local oyster layings, and the halting of shellfish gathering from polluted areas. However, for many years in this century, contagion from excrement—one wretched, horrid stinking closet could be the only resort of twelve families in a tenement—remained everywhere. Between 1982 and 1993, the number of cases each year in the Republic varied from none to four.

Other Insect-Related Health Problems

Allergies

Besides allergies caused by bites and stings (see pages 141-4), allergic reactions can also occur in susceptible people from direct skin contact with certain insects or by inhaling household dust containing their remains. Non-biting midges or chironomids are known to have caused such problems in England and probably have had similar effects in parts of Ireland. When rivers, lakes and reservoirs near residential areas become polluted due to inflowing nutrients, there may be an enormous increase in the numbers of chironomids from spring through to the autumn. Such events have been observed on Lough Neagh and other Irish lakes. The numbers may be large enough to restrict or inhibit human outdoor activities. The chironomids are attracted to light and will readily enter buildings. If hygiene is poor, they will eventually break down and become incorporated into the household dust. Inhalation of this mixture may result in asthma.

Dermestid beetles (Family: Dermestidae) can also cause medical problems. The very hairy larvae easily lose their hairs, and these may cause skin irritation resulting in hives or, if inhaled, inflammation of the nose, eye irritation and asthma. Such medical problems are only likely to occur wherever there are large infestations. Some species infest and eat various woollen textiles (carpets, clothes, curtains, upholstery), furs, hides, feathers and certain food items (especially grain or cereal products). Anyone handling large quantities of infected goods or cargoes may be affected. Toxic problems (enteric canthariasis) can occur if food containing the hairs is eaten.

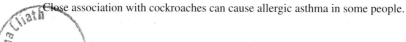

Close association with cockroaches can cause allergic asthma in some people.

Delusory Parasitosis

Throughout our species' history, there has been an uneasy relationship between humans and certain arthropods (insects, spiders, mites and similar creatures). A certain natural revulsion towards insects—which after all may sting, bite, spread disease, contaminate our food—may be perfectly healthy, working, like our natural abhorrence of refuse and excrement, to help maintain high standards of hygiene. Where this wariness of insects becomes more pronounced, however, it may be considered entomophobia, the morbid dread of insects.

When considering household pests, professional eradicators, health inspectors and medical personnel should be aware that in some cases delusory parasitosis or Ekbom's syndrome—where the afflicted person imagines his/her body or house to be infested with numerous invisible biting insects or mites—may be at the root of persistent calls for assistance. Normal procedures of eradication will obviously not solve mainly psychological conditions.

The sufferer experiences an anguished feeling of being unclean and persecuted. It is a very distressing condition for the patient and often involves other members of the family. Eight generalised complaints are listed below as an aid to recognising the condition:

- The 'bugs' are black and white when first noted but may change colour later
- The 'bugs' often infest patient's hair and can be combed out for 'collection'
- The 'bugs' often jump
- 'Bites' on the skin usually itch and cause scratching, sometimes to the point of tissue damage
- The 'bugs' may come from common household products like toothpaste, petroleum jelly or cosmetics
- The 'infestation' can become such a problem that the patient has to move, but the 'bugs' usually reappear in the new dwelling as well
- The patient may be so positive about the infestation and describe it so lucidly that his/her family will often strongly support the patient's claims, even if not affected themselves
- The 'infestation' may have lasted two or three months or longer while actual arthropod infestations seldom last that long.

The great majority of cases seem to involve women, generally middle-aged to elderly, but do also include young men and women. The sufferers are often people of intelligence, who talk rationally except with regard to their unshakable idea of being infested.

Additional symptoms can be also recognised

- a sense of persecution

- frequent attempts at self-medication, sometimes with unpleasant results

- statements that other 'doctors' or 'experts' have been consulted.

The causes of delusory parasitosis may be diverse. Some kind of 'insect shock' is a common precipitating cause. A real infestation (of lice, fleas, or 'bugs') may have previously existed and after it has been cleared up the phobia remains. It is possible that the use of cosmetics or the wearing of synthetic fibres might play a part in promoting the initial symptoms of irritation.

It does not help people suffering from this neurosis to offer them insecticides as a placebo. Instead it is important that they should receive proper medical attention. The entomologist or health inspector should not give medical advice but can advise how such help should be contacted. It is important never to confront the patient with the blunt facts that their 'samples' contain no insects.

Apparently, delusory parasitosis may now be treated with drugs under medical supervision and psychiatric support may also be necessary. When informed, the GP may refer the patient to a dermatologist, who can usually pass him or her on for psychiatric treatment should it prove necessary. Unfortunately, the attitude of many sufferers can make help and treatment difficult.

It is important to stress here that a suspected case of delusory parasitosis may be eventually traceable to real grounds of complaint (such as midge bites, cat fleas, dermatitis due to paint, bed-mites). In one case we have experienced, an actual mite infestation was found only on the fourth examination. It is important therefore to try and establish by every possible means that there is no actual cause for complaint before assuming that the person complaining is suffering from the syndrome.

A bizarre incident occurred recently when a health inspector rang the Natural History Museum concerning crabs in a private house in Dublin city. She said that an elderly householder was deeply worried that crabs were wandering about in her home. At first we thought the lady in question was talking about crab lice, since the matter was being reported to an entomologist, but then it was established that she meant marine crabs. Nevertheless, it sounded remarkably like a case of delusory parasitosis, since the house was in a built-up area some 3.5km from the sea, an unlikely place to find crabs. Surprisingly, it turned out that the householder had true cause for complaint. The submitted specimens were in fact shore-crabs—one of which had been flattened by a thrown telephone book! It is probable that the crabs had originated from an underground river and emerged from the outside drains.

Myiasis

When fly maggots (larvae) feed on or in any part of the body of living animals, this condition is termed 'myiasis'. Fortunately, though farm animals and pets may be infected, myiasis among humans is rare in Ireland. Nevertheless, medical personnel should be aware that these conditions may occur. The parts of the body most commonly affected are as follows:

- The skin and underlying muscle: maggots can rarely penetrate unbroken skin but the more usual method of infection is via wounds, boils or other lesions

- The intestine, where the maggots may have been swallowed in food or drink such as meat, fish, cheese, unwashed vegetables, fruit-juice, alcohol or water, or where the maggots have entered the bowel via the anus

- The urinogenital region, where maggots occur in the urethra, bladder or reproductive system

- The nasopharyngeal region, where maggots live in the nasal passage, sinuses, eyes, ears and, rarely, the mouth or lungs.

It is easy to see how anyone could accidentally swallow maggots by eating infected food or drinking foul water, but it is likely that people suffering from any of the other cases of myiasis have poor hygiene awareness (with cuts and sores left untreated to fester), live in squalid conditions, or are incapable of looking after themselves—such as infants whose soiled nappies are infrequently changed, patients or elderly people in care if hygiene is lax.

Many families of flies have been recorded as causing myiasis and, because indoor pest species are closely associated with humans, these include most of the species of flies covered in this book. However, the most likely culprits are houseflies or bottle flies, since these are opportunists, ready to exploit any suitable situation.

Maggots are an old African treatment for surface ulcers. They clear the dead matter, without harming the living tissue. Currently, a hospital in south Wales is producing medically clean maggots for this purpose.

Appendix 1: Design and Construction

In most parts of the world, including Ireland, major difficulties with insect and other pests have resulted from a combination of inappropriate architectural design, construction faults and the use of unsuitable materials and fittings in buildings, not taking into account that during the life of the structure some pest problems are bound to occur, especially in larger buildings. Design and construction of new buildings and equipment so as to eliminate or minimise harbours and passageways for pests, as well as food accumulations, is known as pest exclusion. Such practices are essential for certain types of buildings including hospitals, hotels, restaurants, schools, apartment blocks and factories, ensuring good hygiene standards or sterile conditions where necessary. Judgement is required, balancing effect against cost.

Many old industrial buildings (flourmills and warehouses, for example) tend to have more serious problems with pests. Stored food, for instance, can become infested by pests flying or crawling in from outside. Thoughtfully designed and carefully constructed structures can assist in eliminating such problems. Careful and permanent sealing of cracks and crevices and other openings will result in a marked reduction. Special attention should be paid to wood-to-wood joints. Doors and windows should be made tight and self-sealing. Incoming goods should be diligently checked to prevent the introduction of pests. Clutter should be avoided or eliminated.

Major pest problems can occur in modern buildings where the design incorporates large amounts of inaccessible empty space in the form of ducts, false ceilings, lift shafts and so on. The various services to different parts of the building are often hidden from view in such places and may consist of water and gas pipes, electrical cables and conduits, air conditioning, ventilation and lift shafts. Insects such as cockroaches will enter these voids freely and exploratory behaviour will take place throughout their lifetime. Infestations can spread throughout a building using these routes.

Serious infestations have been experienced in high-rise apartments in Britain. Cockroaches have been known to invade wall voids in such numbers that continuous masses were formed. False ceilings and wall panelling (usually with a space behind it from floor to ceiling) contribute to the problem. These structures are sometimes connected directly to the spaces containing the various services. When the pests are disturbed or attempts made to eradicate them, some can easily escape into a duct and then quickly recolonise when the danger has passed.

IRISH
INDOOR
INSECTS

Some hints for architects

- False or suspended ceilings should be avoided

- Gaps around pipes, electrical conduits, etc. which pass through walls should be fully sealed with mortar. Seal all crevices. Use tight-fitting doors and windows

- Solid concrete floors on soil at ground level should be sealed with tiles to prevent ants and other insects from entering via cracks in the concrete. With good building practice, there should be no cracks in the concrete, so it is important to inspect the work at all stages

- Avoid the use of skirting boards

- Avoid using cavity blocks, hollow modular and steel units. The sides of the former often have imperfections enabling insects to gain access inside. Insects living inside a large cavity wall are frequently difficult or impossible to locate or exterminate

- Tiling on walls and floors is essential when it is necessary or desirable to clean a room with a steam cleaner

- All furniture and fittings in commercial kitchens should be fitted with wheels to permit thorough cleaning. Sink units should have the taps attached to walls rather than to the mobile unit itself.

Appendix 2: Product Liability Claims

One effect of widespread ignorance about insects is the number of court cases that are taken against companies when minor contaminants are found in food. Awards are often made on the basis of the feelings of disgust or distress expressed by the complainant, but the size of some awards is quite unjustified, since many of the species involved are common in Irish houses and are completely harmless.

Most product liability claims involving insects are not examined scientifically to determine if the claim is valid or not. Many cases would undoubtedly have been dismissed if a professional entomologist had been called to testify on behalf of the defendants. Certainly, large sums would not be paid out unnecessarily, and this in turn would result in lower insurance premiums.

Many problems can be solved at an early stage. If contamination of manufactured or other goods by insects is notified to or detected by a firm, it is advisable to get expert help immediately. The source of the problem may be elsewhere than was originally thought: it may be traced to the raw materials, the manufacturing process, the way in which containers are stored, warehouses, retail outlets or even the home.

Sometimes, consumers do have legitimate complaints which would never have arisen if proper hygiene and quality control practices were in place. After correctly identifying a problem insect, a professional entomologist can usually pinpoint the source of contamination, using information on its life history, behaviour and physical requirements.

Appendix 3: Professional Identification of Insects

Care must be taken to ensure that specimens sent for identification to an entomologist[9] are not damaged or destroyed by improper treatment or packaging. The following guidelines will cover most situations.

Guidelines on packing insects

- You should send several specimens if you have them

- If alive, insects or maggots should be put into a screw-top plastic container along with the food that they were found in

- Dry dead insects should be wrapped loosely in a piece of tissue paper and placed in a plastic container with a lid that can be screwed or secured tightly

- Dead insects found in water or other liquids will easily rot. They should be put in a small plastic bottle which is then filled up with spirits (industrial or laboratory alcohol is usual, but whiskey, gin, vodka or whatever you have in the drinks cabinet will do just as well) to preserve them. Alternatively, freeze the specimen in its bottle until you are ready to send it in

- It is ***not recommended*** to put specimens in match boxes or ordinary envelopes where they can escape or be crushed. It is also not recommended to stick them to sticky tape.

Other points to note

- If you have found an insect in food or drink, keep the bottle, packet, or wrapping and any remaining contents, as they may be required for examination

- Where relevant, note the name of the manufacturer or purchaser, brand name, the dates of complaint, purchase and manufacture, place of purchase and so forth

- If the product is likely to go mouldy or rot, the easiest way to preserve it is to wrap it in a plastic bag and place it in a deep freezer.

9 *An insect identification and report service is provided by SCAN Scientific Analysis, 31 Waterloo Road, Dublin 4 (ph. 01-6681355, fax 01-6681678).*

Glossary of Technical Terms

abdomen: Hindmost of the three main divisions of an insect's body, which may be distinctly or indistinctly divided into segments

annulate: With alternate light and dark ring-like markings

antennae: Pair of jointed, sensory organs or 'feelers' located on the head of an insect. They are very variable in shape, number of joints and structure within the insects and may be long and whip-like (often longer than the body), bushy, branched, feather-like or hair-like, short and simple or even completely absent. Sometimes people mistake the antennae for tails but the head end of a live insect can easily be determined because insects very rarely walk backwards

anterior: Towards the front

apical: Towards the tip or apex of a structure

appendage: Jointed structures on an insect's body (e.g. wings, legs, antennae)

apterous: Wingless

arthropod: Invertebrate animals with segmented bodies, jointed paired appendages (legs, antennae, mouth parts, etc.) and a hard exoskeleton, or skin, made of chitin, for example mites, spiders, insects, ticks, crustaceans (e.g. crabs, shrimps). Spiders, mites and ticks (Arachnida) are incorrectly regarded as insects by many people

aquatic: Living in water

carnivorous: Feeding on live animal prey

caste: Different forms of adult insect within a single species, found among social insects, which perform different tasks within a colony, e.g. queen, drone (male), worker, soldier

caterpillar: Larval stage of butterflies, moths and sawflies

chitin: Hard, horn-like, resistant substance (consisting of a complex carbohydrate) which makes up the external skeleton (and some internal structures) of insects, covering the body like a skin, and acting like a suit of armour for protection

chitinous: Made from chitin

chrysalis (chrysalid): Pupal stage of butterflies and moths

complete metamorphosis: Process of change and growth from egg to adult whereby an insect goes through a number of distinct stages (see pages 2-4)

cuticle: Hard chitinous outer skin of insects

ectoparasite: Parasite (e.g. fleas, lice) that lives and feeds on the body surface (skin, hair, feathers, fur, etc.) of its host animal.

ecosystem: Community of living organisms together with the non-living element which they occupy, e.g. lake, river, desert

egg: First stage in the life-cycle of an insect

elytron (pl. elytra): Hard chitinous modified front wings of beetles and earwigs which protect and cover the delicate flight wings

endoparasite: Parasite that lives and feeds inside the body of its host; e.g. many parasitic wasps are internal parasites of other insects

entomology: Science of the study of insects

entomologist: Person who identifies and studies insects

exuviae: Cast-off older skin of an insect under which, in the course of development, a new skin is grown and which is soon discarded

fauna: All the animal species (insects, worms, birds, mammals, etc.) of a particular area, habitat or region

femur (pl. femora): Third section or division of the leg of insects; usually the largest and most strongly developed part

forceps: 'Pincers' located at the tip of the abdomen in earwigs

frass: Faeces of insects

gall: Abnormal enlargement of plant tissues, caused by an insect or other organism, within which develops the organism or the immature stages of some plant parasitic insects, e.g. gall wasps, gall midges

genal comb: Comb of long spines on the cheeks around the mouth

generation: Time taken to complete development from egg to adult

genitalia: Sexual organs of insects, often used as a way of distinguishing two closely related species

halteres: Pair of club-shaped 'balancers' (highly reduced and modified hind wings) located on the thorax behind the wings of flies (Diptera) and male Coccidae (Hemiptera)

head: First of the three main divisions of an insect's body where the eyes, antennae and mouth parts are located

herbivorous: Feeding exclusively on plants

honeydew: Sweet, sticky liquid waste, excreted through the anus by some plant parasitic insects (especially aphids and scale insects) which other insects are attracted to and feed on. Many ant species farm certain aphid species in order to ensure a steady supply of energy-rich honeydew

host: Plant or animal species upon which an insect parasite feeds or shelters

hyaline: Clear and transparent

imago (pl. imagines): Final stage (adult male or female) in the life-cycle of an insect

incomplete metamorphosis: Process of development whereby an insect changes from a young insect into an adult by moulting several times, but without going through a pupal stage (see pages 2-4).

insect: In the adult stage, segmented invertebrate animals, with three main body divisions (head, thorax, abdomen), with paired jointed appendages (legs, antennae, etc.) and with or without wings

instar: Growth phase in insects between moults; for example, the larva which hatches from the egg is the first instar and when it moults it becomes a second instar larva, and so on

invertebrate: Animal without a backbone, e.g. insects, worms, spiders, molluscs, crustaceans

joint: Articulation or hinge between two adjoining parts which allows movement

larva (pl. larvae): Second stage (after the egg) in the life-cycle of an insect which undergoes complete metamorphosis. Larvae do not resemble adult insects

leather-jackets: Specific term for the larvae of craneflies (Tipulidae - Diptera)

leg: Insect limb divided into a number of sections: coxa, trochanter, femur, tibia and tarsus

maggot: Term applied to the legless larvae, without a distinct head, of some flies (e.g. bluebottle maggots). In Ireland earthworms are sometimes erroneously called maggots

mandibles: Paired, usually toothed structures present in front of the mouth of most insects and used for feeding

metamorphosis: Process of changing from one form or state into another form, e.g. egg to larva, larva to pupa, nymph to adult, pupa to adult

moult: Process of shedding the old body skin, under which a new, soft and larger skin has formed allowing for additional growth

myiasis: Condition whereby the larvae of flies (Diptera) feed on living or dead tissue inside the body of living vertebrate animals (e.g. humans, dogs, sheep, deer) (see page 153).

nocturnal: Active at night only

nymph: Second stage (after the egg) in the life-cycle of insects that undergo incomplete metamorphosis. The nymphs resemble the adults in most features

ootheca: Purse-like egg-cases of some insects (e.g. cockroaches)

oviparous: Egg-producing

oviposit: Lay eggs

ovipositor: Hollow tube-like structure (which may be short or long, fixed or telescopic), located at the end of the abdomen of female insects and used for laying eggs. *Note*: When well developed it is sometimes mistaken for a tail or a sting. However, a sting is actually an ovipositor modified for defence (see *sting*)

palp (pl. palpi): Jointed sensory structure located around the mouth

parasite: Animal or plant which lives on, inside or in association with another animal or plant, e.g. the immature stages of many species of parasitic wasp live inside other insects and develop by feeding on the internal tissues

parthenogenesis: Ability of female insects of some species to produce viable eggs or young without having to mate with a male insect, since in such species sperm for fertilisation of the eggs is not necessary

parthenogenetic species: Insects which are exclusively female (no males exist) and which can produce viable eggs or young

pinaculum (pl. pinacula): One of a set of small plates, which may be white, yellow, brown or black, on the body segments of the larvae of some butterflies and moths

proboscis: Extension, like a snout or beak, of the part of the head that bears the mouth parts

prolegs: Fleshy, unjointed body extensions on the underside of larvae which are used for walking or other purposes. In many caterpillars the first three pairs of legs are jointed legs but all the other 'legs' are prolegs

pronotum: upper surface of prothorax

prothorax: front of thorax

pupa (pl. pupae): Third stage in the life-cycle (after the egg and larval stages) of an insect which undergoes complete metamorphosis. The pupa is a non-feeding stage and is usually well concealed and motionless

puparium: Last larval exuviae or skin which hardens and within which the pupa develops; occurs in some fly species (Diptera)

pupation site: A suitable place to pupate, located by the fully fed last larval stage of some insects, usually a drier, more sheltered place than the food source, and which is safer from predators

saliva: Liquid secretions from the mouth

scales: Modified hairs which are flattened and which completely or partially cover the body of some insects, e.g. moths, butterflies

segments: Ring-like divisions of the bodies of insects which may be clearly or poorly defined

social insects: Insects of a single species which live in nests containing many individuals, ruled by one (or more) queen(s), which work and co-operate together as a community, e.g. the honey bee, many ant species, some wasp species, termites (non-Irish)

sp.: Abbreviation indicating a single distinct species, e.g. *Musca* sp

spp.: Abbreviation indicating two or more distinct species, e.g. *Musca* spp

stigma: Distinct, opaque blackish or brownish mark or spot, usually located along the mid-front of the wings of some insect species

sting: Ovipositor (see above), located at the tip of the abdomen in some insects, which has become highly modified for defence and takes the form of a hollow, needle-like structure which pierces the skin, enabling venom from a sac to enter the wound. Bites, on the other hand are caused by piercing mouthparts (e.g. mosquitoes, bed-bugs, lice), but victims are often not clear about whether they have been stung or bitten

stink glands: Special glands which produce a foul-smelling secretion used as a form of self defence, e.g. some shield bugs, some beetles

tail: Hind part of the abdomen

terrestrial: Living on or in the ground or soil

thorax: Middle part of the three main divisions of an insect's body, located between the head and the abdomen, to which the wings (if present) and legs are attached

vertebrate: Animal with a backbone, e.g. birds, fish, mammals, reptiles, amphibia

viviparous: Describing an insect which produces live young

wing-case: Hard, chitinous front wings, or elytra, of beetles and earwigs, which protect and cover the delicate flight wings

Irish Names for Some Pest Insects

English Name	Irish Name
ant	seangán
aphid	aifid
bacon (or larder) beetle	ciaróg lardrúis
bark beetle	ciaróg choirte
bed bug	míol leapa
bee	beach
beetle	ciaróg
biscuit beetle	ciaróg bhrioscaí
biting midge	míoltóg ghéar
black ant	seangán capaill
black fly	cuil dhubh
bluebottle	cuil ghorm
body louse	míol cnis
booklouse	míol leabhar
brown house-moth	leamhan tí donn
bug	fríd
bumble bee	bumbóg
cabbage (or large) white butterfly	bánóg mhór
carpet beetle	ciaróg olla
case-bearing clothes moth	leamhan éadaigh an cháis
cat flea	dreancaid chait
chafer	deá
cleg	claig
clothes moth	leamhan éadaigh

English Name	*Irish Name*
cluster fly	cnuaschuil
cockchafer	cearnamhán
cockroach	ciaróg
Colorado beetle	ciaróg Cholorado
common clothes moth	leamhan éadaigh
crab louse	míol crúbach
cranefly	galán
daddy-long-legs	fíodóir
death-watch beetle	ciaróg oíche
death's-head hawk-moth	conach na cealtrach
devil's coach-horse	deargadaol
dog flea	dreancaid mhadra
dor beetle	cloigín
earwig	gailseach
firebrat	gilín tine
flea	dreancaid
flesh fly	cuil fheola
flour beetle	ciaróg phlúir
fly	cuil
fruit fly	cuil torthaí
gall wasp	gálfhoiche
garden tiger moth	leamhan tíograch garraí
grasshopper	dreoilín teaspaigh
greenbottle	carrchuil ghlas
greenfly	cuil ghlas
ground beetle	daol
head louse	treaghdán

English Name	Irish Name
hide beetle	ciaróg sheithe
horse fly	creabhar capaill
house cricket	criogar
house fly	cuil tí
human flea	dreancaid duine
human louse	míol duine
ichneumon wasp	foiche icneomónach
kelp fly	ceilpeadóir
lacewing	sciathán lása
larder (or bacon) beetle	ciaróg lardrúis
large (or cabbage) white butterfly	bánóg mhór
locust	lócaiste
longhorn beetle	ciaróg fhadadharcach
louse	míol
louse, body	míol cnis
lousy watchman beetle	cloigín
midge, biting	míoltóg ghéar
midge, non-biting	míoltóg
mosquito	muiscít
moth	leamhan
museum beetle	ciaróg iarsmalainne
parasitic wasp	foiche sheadánach
plaster beetle	ciaróg phlástair
rat-tailed maggot	cruimh eireaballach
red ant	seangán dearg
rove beetle	fándaol
sawfly	sábhchuil

English Name	*Irish Name*
scale insect	feithid ghainneach
scarab beetle	scarab
shield bug	fríd scéithe
silverfish	gilín
solitary wasp	foiche aonair
spider beetle	ciaróg chrúbach
springtail	preabaire
stable fly	cuil stábla
sucking louse	míol súraic
tapestry moth	leamhan taipéise
thrips	tripeas
vinegar fly	cuil fhínéagair
wasp	foiche
wasp, solitary	foiche aonair
water beetle	doirb
weevil	gobachán
whitefly	cuil bhán
white-shouldered house-moth	leamhan tí ceannbhán
woodworm beetle	míol críon

References

This section provides further reading for anyone who wishes to discover more about the various insects. It also cites the works on which much of this book is based.

General References

This section includes both general works and more specialised ones dealing with more than one insect group.

Anon. (1819) *The Natural History of Remarkable Insects with their habits and instincts* (probably edited by Rev. Charles Bardin). William de Veaux, Dublin

Anon. (1967) *Clothes Moths and Carpet Beetles, their Life-history, Habits, and Control.* British Museum (Natural History). Economic series No. **14**: 1-15

Anon. (1974) *Flies and other Insects in Poultry Houses.* Ministry of Agriculture, Fisheries and Food. Advisory leaflet No. **537**: 1–6

Anon. (1977) *Insects and Mites in Farm-stored Grain.* Ministry of Agriculture, Fisheries and Food. Advisory leaflet No. **368**: 1–9

Anon. (1977) *Insect Pests in Food Stores.* Ministry of Agriculture, Fisheries and Food. Advisory leaflet No. **483**: 1–8

Anon. (1978) *Insects infesting Bacon and Hams.* Ministry of Agriculture, Fisheries and Food. Advisory leaflet No. **373**: 1–5

Anon. (1978) *Ainmneacha Plandaí agus Ainmhithe. Fauna and flora nomenclature.* Stationery Office, Dublin.

Aitken, A. D. (1984) *Insect Travellers.* Vol. II. Ministry of Agriculture, Fisheries and Food. Reference Book 437. HMSO, London

Andrews, M. (1976) *The Life that Lives on Man.* Arrow Books, London

Bateman, P. L. G. (1979) *Household Pests.* Blandford Press, Poole

Beirne, B. P. (1952) Insects found in foodstuffs and stored products in Ireland. *Entomologist's Gazette* **3**: 81–84

Brooks, A. & Halstead, A. (1980) *Garden Pests and Diseases. The Royal Horticultural Society's Encyclopaedia of Practical Gardening.* Mitchell Beazley, London

Buczacki, S. & Harris, K. (1983) *Collins Shorter Guide to the Pests, Diseases and Disorders of Garden Plants.* Collins, London

Busvine, J. R. (1975) *Arthropod Vectors of Disease.* Studies in Biology no. 55. Arnold, London

Busvine, J. R. (1980) *Insects and Hygiene.* 3rd edn. Chapman & Hall, London

Chinery, M. (1982) *A Field Guide to the Insects of Britain and Northern Europe.* 2nd edn. Collins, London

Chinery, M. (1986) *Collins Guide to the Insects of Britain and Western Europe.* Collins, London

Frazier, C. A. & Brown, F. K. (1980) *Insects and Allergy, and what to do about them.* University of Oklahoma Press, Norman

Goodhue, D. (1980) *Irish Household Pests.* Folens, Dublin

Gorham, J. R. (ed.) (1991) *Ecology and Management of Food Industry Pests.* FDA Technical Bulletin 4. Association of Official Analytical Chemists, Virginia

Hickin, N. E. (1974) *Household Insect Pests.* Associated Business Programmes, London

Hickin, N. E. (1975) *The Insect Factor in Wood Decay.* Associated Business Programmes, London

Hickin, N. E. (1981) *The Woodworm Problem.* Rentokil, East Grinstead

Hickin, N. E. (1985) *Bookworms, the Insect Pests of Books.* Sheppard Press, London

Hill, D. S. (1975) *Agricultural Insect Pests of the Tropics and their Control.* Cambridge University Press, Cambridge

Lane, R. P. & Crosskey, R. W. (eds) (1993) *Medical Insects and Arachnids.* Chapman & Hall, London

Lydon, J. (1973) *Ireland in the later Middle Ages.* Gill & Macmillan, Dublin

Mound, L. (ed.) (1989) *Common Insect Pests of Stored Food Products.* 7th edn. British Museum (Natural History), London

Mourier, H., Winding, O. & Sunesen, E. (1977) *Collins Guide to Wildlife in House and Home.* Collins, London

Munro, J. W. (1966) *Pests of Stored Products.* Hutchinson, London

Nash, R. & O'Connor, J. P. (1990) Insects imported into Ireland 9. Records of Orthoptera, Dictyoptera, Homoptera and Hymenoptera including Roger's ant, *Hypoponera punctatissima* (Roger). *Irish Naturalists' Journal* **23**: 255–7

O'Brien, J. V. (1982) *"Dear, dirty Dublin". A City in Distress, 1899–1916.* Macmillan, London

O'Connor, J. P. (1983) Have you come across delusory parasitosis? *Yearbook of the Environmental Health Officers' Association* **1983**: 61–3

O'Connor, J. P. (1983) Notes on insect pests received for identification by the National Museum of Ireland. *Bulletin of the Irish Biogeographical Society* **5**: 5–14

O'Connor, J. P. (1984) Notes on insect pests received for identification by the National Museum of Ireland: a second report. *Bulletin of the Irish Biogeographical Society* **7**: 38–44

O'Connor, J. P. & Nash, R. (1979) Records of six insect species (Coleoptera: Orthoptera) recently imported into Ireland. *Irish Naturalists' Journal* **19**: 433–4

O'Connor, J. P. & Nash, R. (1983a) Insects imported into Ireland 5. Records of Orthoptera, Hemiptera, Hymenoptera and Coleoptera. *Irish Naturalists' Journal* **21**: 114–17

O'Connor, J. P. & Nash, R. (1983b) Insects imported into Ireland 6. Records of Orthoptera, Dermaptera, Lepidoptera and Coleoptera. *Irish Naturalists' Journal* **21**: 351–3

O'Connor, J. P. & Nash, R. (1986) Insects imported into Ireland 8. Records of Hemiptera, Coleoptera, Diptera and Lepidoptera. *Irish Naturalists' Journal* **22**: 104–7

O'Connor, J. P., Ashe, P., O'Neill, L., Bond, K. G. M. & Murray, D. A. (1990) Some insect pests which recently caused public concern in Ireland. *Bulletin of the Irish Biogeographical Society* **13**: 141–65

O'Farrell, A. F. & Butler, P. M. (1948) Insects and mites associated with the storage and manufacture of foodstuffs in Northern Ireland. *Economic Proceedings of the Royal Dublin Society* **3**: 343–407

Pinniger, D. (1994) *Insect Pests in Museums.* 3rd edn. Archetype Publications, London

Ryan, J. G., O'Connor, J. P. & Beirne, B. P. (1984) *A Bibliography of Irish Entomology*. Fly Leaf Press, Dublin

Seymour, P. R. (1989) *Invertebrates of Economic Importance in Britain. Common and Scientific Names*. Ministry of Agriculture, Fisheries and Food. 4th edn. HMSO, London

Smith, K. G. V. (ed.) (1973) *Insects and other Arthropods of Medical Importance*. British Museum (Natural History), London

Smith, K. G. V. (1986) *A Manual of Forensic Entomology*. British Museum (Natural History), London

Zinsser, H. (1963, reprinted 1985) *Rats, Lice and History. The Biography of a Bacillus*. Macmillan, London

Zumpt, F. (1965) *Myiasis in Man and Animals in the Old World*. Butterworths, London

Small Orders and True Bugs—(Order: Hemiptera)

Blackman, R. (1974) *Aphids*. Ginn, London

Dolling, W. R. (1991) *The Hemiptera*. Oxford University Press, Oxford

Lehane, B. (1969) *The Compleat Flea*. Murray, London

Marshall, J. A. & Haes, E. C. M. (1988) *Grasshoppers and Allied Insects of Great Britain and Ireland*. Harley Books, Colchester

Mound, L. A. & Halsey, S. H. (1978) *Whitefly of the World*. British Museum (Natural History), London

Mound, L. A., Morison, G. D., Pitkin, B. R. & Palmer, J. M. (1976) Thysanoptera. *Handbooks for the Identification of British Insects* **1** (11): 1–79

Nash, R., Boston, M. R., Black, T. B. & O'Connor, J. P. (1985) Insects imported into Ireland 7. The brown-banded cockroach *Supella supellectilium* (Serville). *Irish Naturalists' Journal* **21**: 495–6

New, T. R. (1974) Psocoptera. *Handbooks for the Identification of British Insects* **1** (7): 1–102

O'Connor, J. P. & Smithers, C. N. (1982) An Irish record of the booklouse *Badonnelia titei* Pearman (Psocoptera, Sphaeropsocidae). *Entomologist's Monthly Magazine* **118**: 226

O'Connor, J. P. & Smithers, C. N. (1987) *Badonnelia titei* Pearman (Psocoptera, Sphaeropsocidae); a splendid addition to the library of the National Museum of Ireland. *Entomologist's Monthly Magazine* **123**: 125

Palmer, J. M., Mound, L. A. & de Heaume, G. J. (1989). *Thysanoptera*. CAB International, Oxon

Rothschild, M. & Clay. T. (1953) *Fleas, Flukes and Cuckoos*. Collins, London

Southwood, T. R. E. & Leston, D. (1959) *Land and Water Bugs of the British Isles*. Warne, London

Moths and Butterflies—(Order: Lepidoptera)

Carter, D. J. (1984) Pest Lepidoptera of Europe with special reference to the British Isles. *Series Entomologica* **31**: 1–431 Junk, Dordrecht

Corbet, A. S. & Tams, W. H. T. (1943) Keys for the identification of the Lepidoptera infesting stored food products. *Proceedings of the Zoological Society of London*, (B) **118**: 55–148

Goater, B. (1986) *British Pyralid Moths. A Guide to their Identification*. Harley Books, Colchester

Holloway, J. D., Bradley, J. D. & Carter, D. J. (1987) *Lepidoptera*. CAB International, Oxon

Ants, Bees and Wasps—(Order: Hymenoptera)

Bolton, B. & Collingwood, C. A. (1975) Hymenoptera Formicidae. *Handbooks for the Identification of British Insects* **6** (3c): 1–34

Edwards, R. (1980) *Social Wasps. Their Biology and Control*. Rentokil, East Grinstead

Gauld, I. & Bolton, B. (eds) (1988) *The Hymenoptera*. British Museum (Natural History), London & Oxford University Press, Oxford

Beetles—(Order: Coleoptera)

Aitken, A. D. (1975) *Insect Travellers*. Vol. I. Ministry of Agriculture, Fisheries and Food. Technical Bulletin 31. HMSO, London

Booth, R. G., Cox, M. L. & Madge, R. B. (1990) *Coleoptera*. International Institute of Entomology, London

Brendell, M. J. D. (1975) Coleoptera Tenebrionidae. *Handbooks for the Identification of British Insects* **5** (10): 1–22

Good, J. A. & Ashe, P. (1990) Records of four species of false powder-post beetle (Coleoptera: Bostrichidae: *Dinoderus*) imported into Ireland. *Irish Naturalists' Journal* **8**: 326–7

Hall, D. W. & Howe, R. W. (1953) A revised key to the larvae of the Ptinidae associated with stored products. *Bulletin of Entomological Research* **44**: 85–96

Harde, K. W. (1984) *A Field Guide in Colour to Beetles*. Octopus Books, London

Hinton, H. E. (1945) *A Monograph of the Beetles Associated with Stored Products*. British Museum (Natural History), London

O'Connor, J. P. (1978a) Occurrence of *Euophryum rufum* Broun (Col., Curculionidae) in Ireland. *Entomologist's Monthly Magazine* **113**: 56

O'Connor, J. P. (1978b) An Irish record of the hide beetle *Dermestes carnivorus* F. (Col., Dermestidae). *Entomologist's Monthly Magazine* **113**: 150

Flies—(Order: Diptera)

Ashe, P., O'Connor, J. P. & Casey, R. J. (1991) Irish mosquitoes (Diptera: Culicidae): a checklist of the species and their known distribution. *Proceedings of the Royal Irish Academy* **91B**: 21–36

Colyer, C. N. & Hammond, C. O. (1968) *Flies of the British Isles*. 2nd edn (revised). Warne, London

Cranston, P. S., Ramsdale, C. D., Snow, K. R. & White, G. B. (1987) Adults, larvae and pupae of British mosquitoes (Culicidae). *Scientific Publications of the Freshwater Biological Association* **48**: 1–152

Nash, R. & O'Connor, J. P. (1982) *Limnophora exuta* and *Leptocera caenosa* (Insecta: Diptera) new to Ireland. *Irish Naturalists' Journal* **20**: 549–50

O'Connor, J. P. & Ashe, P. (1992) *Drosophila repleta* Wollaston (Dipt., Drosophilidae), an unsavoury find in a Dublin pub. *Entomologist's Monthly Magazine* **128**: 146

O'Connor, J. P. & Sleeman, D. P. (1987) A review of the Irish Hippoboscidae (Insecta: Diptera). *Irish Naturalists' Journal* **22**: 236–9

Oldroyd, H. (1964) *The Natural History of Flies*. Weidenfeld & Nicolson, London

Shorrocks, B. (1972) *Drosophila*. Ginn, London

Smith, K. G. V. (1989) An introduction to the immature stages of British Flies. Diptera larvae, with notes on eggs, puparia and pupae. *Handbooks for the Identification of British Insects* **10** (14): 1–280

Index